Resilience: Going Within in a Time of Crisis

The *Resilience* Series

Resilience:
Going Within in a
Time of Crisis

P.T. Mistlberger

CHANGEMAKERS
BOOKS

Winchester, UK
Washington, USA

JOHN HUNT PUBLISHING

First published by Changemakers Books, 2020
Changemakers Books is an imprint of John Hunt Publishing Ltd., No. 3 East Street,
Alresford, Hampshire SO24 9EE, UK
office@jhpbooks.com
www.johnhuntpublishing.com
www.changemakers-books.com

For distributor details and how to order please visit the 'Ordering' section on our website.

A CIP catalogue record for this book is available from the British Library.

Design: Stuart Davies

UK: Printed and bound by CPI Group (UK) Ltd, Croydon, CR0 4YY
Printed in North America by CPI GPS partners

We operate a distinctive and ethical publishing philosophy in
all areas of our business, from our global network of authors to
production and worldwide distribution.

Contents

Acknowledgements

My thanks to Tim Ward, publisher of Changemakers Books, for asking me to write this short book under an equally short deadline. Tim, with his usual tenacity, hacked and hewed at my first draft until there was almost nothing left. Then mysteriously and Phoenix-like, there arose from the ashes a second draft, which became the book you now hold in your hands. My thanks also to John Hunt, founder of John Hunt Publishing, the parent company, as well as to the fine production team at JHP, and to the other authors of the *Resilience* series of books of which this title is one. May the force be with them all.

Foreword: *Resilience In a Time of Crisis*

"What can we do to help?"

In a time of crisis - such as the 2020 covid-19 pandemic - we all have a natural impulse to help our neighbors. John Hunt, founder of John Hunt Publishing, asked this question of our company, and then offered a suggestion. He proposed producing a series of short books written by experts offering practical, emotional, and spiritual skills to help people survive in the midst of a crisis.

To reach people when they need it most, John wanted to accomplish this in forty days. Bear in mind, the normal process of bringing a book from concept to market takes at least eighteen months. As publisher of the JHP imprint Changemakers Books, I volunteered to execute this audacious plan. My imprint publishes books about personal and social transformation, and I already knew many authors with exactly the kinds of expertise we needed. That's how the *Resilience* series was born.

I was overwhelmed by my authors' responses. Ten of them immediately said yes and agreed to the impossible deadline. The book you hold in your hands is the result of this intensive, collaborative effort. On behalf of John, myself, the authors and production team, our intention for you is that you take to heart the skills and techniques offered to you in these pages. Master them. Make yourself stronger. Share your newfound resilience with those around you. Together, we can not only survive, but learn how to thrive in tough times. By so doing, we can find our way to a better future.

Tim Ward
Publisher, Changemakers Books
May 1, 2020

In a dark time, the eye begins to see.
—Theodore Roethke

People wish to be settled. Only as far as they are unsettled, is there any hope for them.
—Emerson

Introduction

I was invited to write this short book by my publisher in light of the challenging crisis of 2020, the global novel coronavirus pandemic. The book that follows is not about that event, but rather about our psychological responses to a crisis of any order of magnitude, from getting fired from a job, ending a relationship, or something more large-scale. The premise of this book is that during a time of crisis—and especially one that involves some variation of physical distancing—the ability to 'go within' becomes crucial for well-being.

There are of course many practical ways to 'go within' in the context of work on self. Some involve different forms of meditation, some involve art therapy or journaling. Some also involve simple contemplation. There are also forms of 'going within' that are less that, than they are idle day-dreaming, or excessive rumination. It is common, for example, when feeling stressed, to dwell on old memories, not all of which may be pleasant. The present book is concerned with productive and illuminating ways of going within.

Since approximately the mid-1990s the Internet has been widely used, and today, a quarter of a century later, online life is so intertwined with our daily existence that for younger folk it is almost hard to imagine (or remember, for older folk) when such a thing did not exist. This may seem to indicate that our collective society, and people in general, have grown more introverted. I would argue however that this is more an artificial introversion, where people are more commonly staring at screens than they are truly looking into their minds.

In this short book I will outline some teachings and guidelines for going within, based on my many decades of making this inner journey. The main point I want to stress here off the top is that 'going within' during a time of crisis—which includes a global crisis—is not about avoiding responsibilities or relationships. It is not about an insular, self-congratulatory practice that ignores the plight of others. On the contrary, it is about using one's time to look more closely in the psychological mirror and develop the correct attitude in the face of hardship, even while we do whatever is necessary to deal with worldly necessities and keep our relationships clear and balanced.

As I write these words in the spring of 2020, the exponentially growing statistics concerning the novel coronavirus, on a global level, have been disturbing and stressful to many. Listing the numbers at present seems pointless as they are increasing daily in many countries (even as they level off, and begin to decline, in others). The medical realities have been made clear by the experts, but these have also been accompanied by economic realities, and difficult financial stresses incurred by many. For all of us, 2020 is an unprecedented year. The last great pandemic of a similar nature, with a significant loss of life, was just over a century ago. Few, if any, are alive who have personal memories of that event.

Why Go Within?

One argument in support of the importance of going within during a time of crisis is to turn away from thinking that is fueled by anxiety. This kind of thinking plays havoc with our minds, because it is usually seeking some sort of explanation for the anxiety we feel. We may think we find this in dwelling on outer circumstances, such as individuals or organizations or governments to blame, or conditions to fret about. And in larger-scale crises, such as the global pandemic of 2020, some might even take refuge in conspiracy theories, which appear to offer up select bogie men to pin the cause of everything on. That might seem to be a short-term fix for our anxiety, but it is usually based on a lack of critical thinking and the desire to turn the unknown into the known—better the devil you know, than the devil you don't. It is in the very nature of a crisis, of any order of magnitude, to bring about changes, and such changes inevitably are accompanied by uncertainty and the unknown. Conspiracy theories may appear to offer up shelter from facing our anxieties and the unknown before us, but in addition to usually being factually wrong, they also generally do not contribute toward well-being and a balanced state of mind.

Going within, in the sense that I mean it in this book, is an attempt to take stock of our mind, and utilize some time-honored methods to work with our mind during such times.

Hard Times and Resilience

As just mentioned, this book is not about a global pandemic. That said, a brief overview of some previous similar global events of disastrous magnitude can be useful to summarize, if only to provide broader context. We humans are deeply resilient creatures by nature. You could say that resilience is baked into our DNA. We have been around—in our current form as *homo sapiens*—for at least 300,000 years, and probably as far back as 500,000 years.[1] Our anatomical ancestors (such as *homo habilis*) go back even further in the fossil record, as far back as two million years, with even older ancestral species beyond that. So clearly, the force of Nature is strong in modern humans, drawing on thousands of centuries of natural selection to result in a tough and resilient species. We have that going in our favor. But when caught up in the throes of our particular crisis, it's easy to forget that bigger picture.

A rough breakdown of pandemics in the past hundred years or so looks like this:

1. 1918 Spanish flu pandemic (so-called only because it was first reported by the Spaniards, not because it began there): This was an H1N1 flu. It infected about 500

million, or about one-third of the global population at that time. The mortality estimate of the 1918 pandemic varies greatly, running anywhere between 20 and 100 million killed. Fatality rate was around 2%, which gives it the maximum 'five' rating on the Pandemic Severity Index.[2] It burned out after about 18 months, possibly due to increasing lack of hosts (deaths, plus herd immunity, which occurs when enough people recover and develop antibodies to the virus). At the time of the 1918 pandemic, there were no vaccines and antibiotics to treat secondary bacterial infections. We did not even yet understand how viruses caused diseases. The Spanish flu spread through respiratory droplets and attacked mainly younger people under 40.

2. Asian influenza pandemic of 1957–58. Killed over 1 million worldwide. About 90,000 died in the U.S.

3. Hong Kong influenza of 1968–69. Killed around 1 million worldwide. Both the Asian flu and the Hong Kong flu were of category 2 severity, meaning they killed around 0.5% of people afflicted. By comparison, the seasonal flu is a category 1, with a less than 0.1% fatality rate.

4. The SARS virus (which is a type of coronavirus) emerged from China in 2002. While its effects could be severe, it did not survive long in the global population and afflicted just over 8,000 people worldwide. However, it had a lethal fatality rate, killing 9%, or close to 700 people. The SARS pandemic ended in the summer of 2003, when the vaccine also became available.

5. The H1N1 flu pandemic of 2009–2010 emerged out of Mexico, and ultimately afflicted about one-quarter of

all people on Earth, or around 1.7 billion people. The fatality rate was comparatively low, just 0.02%, with around 284,000 dying. As a comparative example, the 2020 coronavirus is, as of April, showing about a 2% to 3% fatality rate.[3]

6. Ebola. This lethal virus was first detected in late 2013 in New Guinea but didn't appear as an outbreak until the spring of 2014. It was concentrated mainly in West Africa, afflicting close to 29,000 people and killing in excess of 11,000 of them. Those struck with this virus had a 40% to 50% chance of dying. For that reason, it was the most frightening of the viruses listed here, even if it was nowhere near as contagious as the others. Minor outbreaks have continued in various African countries up to 2019.

Far greater disease-based calamities can be found throughout history, such as the Black Death of the mid-14th century, a version of the bubonic plague, in which roughly half of the entire population of Europe was killed off between 1347–51, and which recurred periodically after that over the next three centuries.

Great crises, on a global scale, have been consistent throughout history. In the 21st century alone, these have been some of the worst ones:

- The September 2001, terrorist attacks on the World Trade Towers, resulting in close to 3,000 deaths.
- The 2003 European heat wave, a summer that recorded the hottest temperatures in Europe since the 16th century. The heat wave killed over 70,000 people.
- The Indian Ocean earthquake of December 2004, which triggered a series of 100-foot-high tsunamis, ultimately killing about 228,000 people in 14 countries bordering the

Indian Ocean.

- Hurricane Katrina, which devastated much of New Orleans in August of 2005 and killed over 1,200.
- Haiti earthquake of 2010, which killed around 150,000, though possibly more.
- The Great Japan earthquake of 2011, along with accompanying tsunamis, killed over 16,000 people, with another 2,500 missing (and is considered the costliest natural disaster in history).

These large-scale crises are utterly beyond the control of the individual, but the fears provoked by our personal, small-scale crises can seem every bit as strong, if not more so.

The Illusion of Control

Diseases and natural disasters are distinct from man-made wars, and yet in the end all of them bear the marks of mega-events beyond any semblance of personal control. We humans live, to some extent, lives founded on elaborately constructed illusions, one of which is the idea that we are somehow in control of things. Smaller scale, personal crises, usually involve the theme of losing control, something commonly reflected in dreams at night involving themes of being out of control (a car with no breaks, a plane that flies crazily, a journey through some huge and frightening landscape, being caught naked in public, and so forth).

The great teacher from the East known as the Buddha based his teachings mainly on the understanding that the individual self is largely an elaborate mental construction. . We have the remarkable ability to live out our lives within the parameters of this illusion, but we also, more problematically, regularly experience all the suffering that comes along with the deeply ingrained belief that we exist as truly separate selves. A global crisis, as well as an individual crisis, hammers hard on this carefully constructed worldview that we are all separate—from each other, from other nations, and from the planet itself.

Whenever our sense of self along with its most cherished illusions is threatened, we typically experience fear in any one of its many faces. The fear largely reduces to some form of *fear of the unknown*. This unknown may take very practical forms, such as not knowing how bills will be paid in the event of job losses or other economic shortfalls, or even how food will be put on our table or on the table of those we support, care for, or care about. It may even take form as fear of our own mortality.

In this connection, the etymology of the English word 'crisis' is interesting and revealing. It stems from the Greek word *krisis*, which means 'turning point in a disease'. It speaks to the proverbial fork in the road, in which the disease could get better or worse, and therefore decisions made at that time are crucial. 'Disease' here is best understood as both physical and mental. For our very real physical realities are always accompanied by psychological realities that, on occasion, can be as bad or even worse. Dealing with those psychological realities becomes crucial to our well-being. This is true whether we are physically ill or not or whether our crisis is related to something different and unexpected altogether.

A key to moving beyond the fear of the unrecognized or unknown, is via the spaciousness of our mind that tends to occur when confronted by the unknown. This spaciousness occurs because our normal train of thought tends to slow down or get stopped altogether. If we don't yield to fear, there is then the possibility of doing real visionary work. That is, allowing fresh new thoughts and visions of future possibilities enter us that we might never have considered if our world had not been rocked by a crisis.

Chapter 1

Going Within #1: Nightfall and the Fear of the Unknown

In early 1941, the renowned 20th century American science fiction author Isaac Asimov published an apocalyptic short story called *Nightfall*. The premise of the story is relatively straightforward. It centers on an alien solar system that has several suns (as opposed to our own system, which has only one star). In that solar system is a planet, populated with intelligent humanoid life.

This alien planet, with its several suns, is bathed in perpetual sunlight, and never knows the night—except for once every two thousand years, when a very rare eclipse and solar configuration occurs that results in an actual night. There are myths and legends about this nightfall, which include the idea (preposterous to the denizens) that with nightfall will appear all these stars in the sky. They have of course never seen stars, which only show at night (something they have not known in their lifetime), and so the existence of these 'stars' is considered by them to be pure myth.

In the story, a journalist visits a group of scientists who warn him of an impending danger brought on by a doomsday scenario. They based their warning on studies of ancient civilizations, all of which appeared to collapse into self-destructive chaos at periodic intervals of about every two thousand years. They believe that the next cycle may soon be upon them.

The further disturbing fact recognized by the scientists is that each of these past civilizations appeared to destroy themselves via fire. The reason for this becomes clear as the story works toward its conclusion. The day—or more precisely, the *night*—comes when the prophesied nightfall really does occur, as the rare astronomical phenomenon of five of the suns facing one side of the planet, with the sixth sun being eclipsed by a previously undetected moon, happens.

The basic premise of the story is that the people of this planet will not be able to handle the psychological effects of nightfall, and civilization will collapse in panic and chaos. When the eclipse occurs, and the nightfall descends, many of the inhabitants of the planet do in fact go insane.

The singular question on everyone's mind in the alien civilization, prior to the rare event, is how its people will react. Even as Asimov was formulating the story, he had wondered about this. At the top of his story he ended up quoting the great American philosopher Emerson, who in the 19th century had written,

If the stars should appear one night in a thousand years, how would men believe and adore, and preserve for many generations the remembrance of the city of God! [4]

John W. Campbell, Asimov's equally famous publisher, had begged to differ with Emerson. He suspected that people would probably lose their sanity. Asimov was influenced by Campbell's view and it became a key piece to his story—the psychological failure of people to adapt to the unknown.

In the story, when the planet is plunged into darkness and nightfall begins, thousands of stars overhead appear. No one alive on the planet has ever seen such a thing, and neither has any ancestor in living memory. The sight is utterly alien to them, and to many of the population, because they are not biologically or psychologically adapted to night, gradually it becomes terrifying and unsustainable.

To ratchet up the intensity, Asimov has the alien world in the middle of a major globular cluster, where stars are packed relatively close together. As a result, the night sky is brilliant and intense with the light of thirty thousand stars, or about ten times as many as are visible on an average night on Earth.

To escape their crippling fear of the dark and the incomprehensible starlight overhead, the natives of the planet begin to create fires, in order to generate more light. Their cities begin to burn, and the cycle of disaster is repeated one more time as the planet plunges into chaos. The story ends with the line, *The long night had come again.*

We are, at the time of the global pandemic of 2020, also in a type of long night. At this point, we are also unsure of how long it will last. The effects of this 'long night' may not be known for some time. But one thing has always been notable throughout history, and that is that during dark times, people acquire other abilities, one of which is to adapt to the darkness.

The stars at night drove many of the inhabitants of Asimov's world mad because they represented the full force of the *unknown*. There is little in life that terrifies us more than the unknown. People will commonly choose the *known hell* over the unknown (which is why negative patterns are so utterly repetitive). And yet, the essence of waking up to higher possibility and the vast potential of our deeper nature lies in embracing the unknown.

Sooner or later we all need to face the searing light of the stars at night, all the more so if we have never allowed for the possibility that they, just like our higher potential, even exist.

Asimov wrote his story at a time when a great upheaval was already occurring on planet Earth. We were already one year into the Second World War. Just two months after *Nightfall* was published the Japanese attacked Pearl Harbor and America was shocked into a direct and painful encounter with its own version of the unknown. *Nightfall* hit on the zeitgeist of its time and struck a note that was strangely familiar to many of its readers. (And it was not the only science fiction tale that was eerily prescient: H.G.Wells' 1897 story *The War of the Worlds* featured alien invaders who were killed off by a pathogen to which they had no natural immunity).

Large-scale events, such as wars or pandemics, can shock

people into one of two directions: toward more awareness, or toward more unconsciousness. The stars in Asimov's story can also be understood as symbols for our inner world as well. When the lights go out in our world—when a crisis of some sort occurs—we can truly look within. If what we see scares us, we run, pushed by all our anxieties, toward creating 'artificial lights'—the many distractions of our life. Alternatively, we might simply bear witness to these stars and come to know them and even understand them. We might just *adapt*.

Times of crisis and difficulty tend to be very revealing. Above all, they reveal where we are out of balance—both with ourselves, with others in our life, and with our world at large. To truly look within, to *go* within, is to stay in balance with the world around us by connecting with the natural silence and energy that lies, like a hidden power source, within. The world of our technological tools, our computers and smartphones and TVs and endless platforms of communication and entertainment, if over-indulged in, pull us out of ourselves, into realms of excessive information and even subtle states of hypnosis. Going within, in a skillful fashion, keeps us sane in insane times.

Chapter 2

Going Within #2: Examining Compulsion and Anxiety

During difficult times—either individual or collective crises—there is always the opportunity to pay closer attention to what is around us. This includes not just our immediate environment and society, as well as our relationships, but also, and most crucially, our own body and mind. Unfortunately, when fear arises in the face of the unknowns that typically accompany a crisis, we commonly resort to patterns that can best be defined as compulsions. Although the opportunity is ripe to be more conscious, we commonly become less so.

The word 'compulsion' derives from the Latin *compellere*, meaning to 'drive' or 'force'. It's a word that has been in usage for centuries. It wasn't until 1909 when the word began to be used to describe a psychological state, one involving rigid behaviors enacted to prevent distressing feelings from arising. Essentially, this kind of compulsiveness is an attempt to block anxiety.

The pathological state of compulsion, usually termed 'obsessive-compulsive', may be well recognized, but what is less commonly acknowledged is how this kind of behavior is enacted by average people in a fashion that is mainly unrecognized. This 'low-grade' compulsiveness is usually dismissed as a manifestation of the person's character or blamed on their circumstances if we are sympathetic toward them.

In times of crisis, people commonly experience anxiety. In dealing with the uncertainty of the future, and any anxieties that may arise with that uncertainty, we typically begin to counter this anxiety via some form of control. In specific, by some form of compulsive behavior.

Compulsive behavior is mechanical, based on acting out

routines. In people with a recognized pathology, the behavior in question will seem obvious, especially to those who know the person well. But in the cases of most people who are overly controlling or functionally compulsive, these behaviors are not necessarily obvious at all. They more commonly tend to be accepted by others, if they are even noticed. And when they are noticed, they are often not objected to, for any number of reasons.

When a large-scale crisis occurs, there is both an individual and a collective calling to something greater. This calling can only be answered, however, if we are not controlled by self-centered instincts. These instincts are primal and geared toward helping us survive. But they can easily over-function. Below are some examples.

1. Avoiding issues. Instead of turning inward to face the issues in life we need to deal with, we turn away from them, into outer distractions, using the crisis we are caught up in as an excuse. 'I'll handle it later, when I'm ready'. This statement only rarely has any basis in clarity. More commonly we *never* feel completely ready to face into difficult issues. Rather, the issues themselves gradually transform as we muster the resolve to face into them. This requires truly going within, in order to take stock of our perspectives in life.

2. Clinging to faulty positions. Nietzsche once famously wrote,
   'A very popular error: having the courage of one's convictions. Rather it is a matter of having the courage for an attack on one's convictions.' [5]

The importance of these words can't be overestimated. There is a reason why pride has so typically been associated with downfall or sooner or later meeting up with a bad fate. A major cause

15

of human suffering is related to holding on to fixed positions in the mind and being unwilling to open to a greater or even just different viewpoint. A crisis often shakes the foundations of our beliefs and viewpoints. It requires courage to look within and take stock of these beliefs and viewpoints and recognize whether we hold on to them merely as a point of pride. If we do hold onto them because we are too proud to let go of them, this almost always leads to suffering, both individually, and commonly for those around us. If we hold a position of power in the world—whether on a large scale, or even if we run a small business with a few employees—it can easily lead to suffering for them as well.

The reason it leads to suffering is because we are not purely fighting for our viewpoints, we are more truly fighting for our *identity*, which is based on our views of life. This is why people will feel so threatened or even fight to the death when their beliefs are assailed (with perhaps the worst examples being in partisan politics and fundamentalist religion). It is rarely the content of their beliefs that they fight over, it is more their personal identification with and emotionally based right to hold these beliefs and positions, in the face of anything.

Convictions: I am Right and you are Wrong

Most commonly in life we can get along fine holding on to dubious convictions, because usually it is a private matter and we humans are granted a measure of natural privacy, if only in the corridors of our mind. But a crisis has a way of changing everything. A deep crisis, such as a national or global event, is often called the Great Equalizer, because it doesn't discriminate and operates with mindless indifference. In the face of this impersonal power, our convictions often get rocked, sometimes hard. The golden opportunity there is to examine these convictions and see them for what they really are.

If we realize that some of these viewpoints have been holding us back, we have the chance to move beyond them. We don't even necessarily have to 'attack' them, as Nietzsche exhorts. We might just discard them. And a major element of these viewpoints is often related to the belief in our specialness. The Great Equalizer of a large-scale, or personal, crisis, tends to knock down or even destroy outright our attachments to believing we are special in some way that marks us apart from the human condition or the mass of humanity. We soon discover that we are not special in that way. In the face of this realization, we are faced with a fork in the road: one way leads toward compulsive ego-based routines and habits that sink us deeper into unconsciousness, the other way leads toward wakefulness and the expansion of our heart, and the recognition that we are truly connected to everything. The 2020 global pandemic tagline 'we are all in this together', speaks to this.

3. Identity and the Unknown. The main defining feature of all traditions concerned with the matter of becoming more awake ultimately centers on the issue of the nature of identity. The sense of *personal* identity is perhaps the essential mystery of existence. When thoughts arise in the mind, the first inclination is to regard them as 'my' thoughts; that is, to assume that such thoughts relate to an individual personality and thinker who is somehow 'thinking' these thoughts.

It is remarkably straightforward to see the flaw in this notion. All we have to do is summon the discipline to quietly pay attention to our thoughts, and in particular, to the moment that they appear to arise in our awareness. One moment we are not thinking a thought, and the next moment, we are. From where did the thought originate? And who (or what) is this mysterious 'me' that is somehow in the background, causing a particular thought to appear?

Taking Things Personally

A reasonable period of sustained focus on this mystery will soon reveal that the issue is not the matter of the origin of any particular thought. The issue is the matter of the belief in some discrete entity in the background who is somehow causing these thoughts to appear. This 'entity' — what we commonly identify as our ego-self — is very vulnerable, and prone to taking things personally.

The tendency to 'take things personally' is an enormous problem in life for many people. Times of crises often stir up vulnerabilities and fears connected to survival, and our ability to function and support ourselves and others. Much of this connects to our fears of how others perceive us. The fear of being judged is more or less a universal fear, especially for younger people. Public speaking is intimidating for many, because it is the fullest demonstration of receiving focused attention from others. If we harbour thoughts that we are unworthy, inadequate, and so on, then there will be a corresponding fear of being judged and found wanting by these others who are giving us their attention.

The fear of being judged is related to self-importance . We can only be afraid of being judged if we somehow believe that we are special in some way, important in some way that defines us as essentially different from others. In this context, 'self-importance' is not to be confused with 'good self-esteem'; the latter is merely a natural state in which we do not encounter any significant inner blocks to expressing ourselves in a healthy and natural fashion. The Sun shines naturally; so too is a human individual meant to 'shine naturally', simply by doing what comes naturally to them.

The deeper point is that we fear the judgments of others because we ourselves are consumed by judgments, both of others, and of ourselves. (And the 'judgment' spoken of here should not be confused with *discernment*, which is a different function, one indeed necessary for navigating a world of space, time, and bodies—outwardly in physical details, inwardly in our personal development). Egocentric judgment reinforces self-importance (and indeed, arises from it). Self-importance, in turn, is based on the mistaken view that the thoughts that arise in our mind all relate centrally back to a discrete 'me' that is, in fact, generating these thoughts.

A close examination of the matter of where thoughts are arising from (or 'who', for that matter, is creating them), does not yield any insight into some 'thought-creator'. Rather, it yields something infinitely more humbling—a direct glimpse into the unknowable ground of consciousness from which all forms, appearances, and thoughts arise. This 'ground' is not anything, and so naturally cannot ultimately give rise to any discrete things (including individuals). All that exists are the endless *appearances* of such. There is freedom in this insight and help in lifting the burden of egocentric perspective. To see deeply into this, by going within and examining our thoughts, leads eventually to the comforting realization that we are not that important in the greater scheme of things. The world is not waiting with bated breath for our very next action.

That does *not* mean, however, that our life has no meaning. On the contrary, it has great meaning, and our personal contribution to the human race and the planet *is* important, precisely because each of us is utterly unique. But we are not more, or less, important than others. Like infinite shades of colors in a refracted rainbow, each unique, we are all—in our deepest essence—pure light on the other side of the prism.

Psychological suffering, in all its many faces of compulsion and anxieties and a whole raft of negative emotions, occurs in proportion to the degree that we think we are someone separate and distinct from the Whole—all the while seemingly producing thoughts that also appear to be separate and distinct from the Whole. This ego-constructed edifice typically takes a beating, or comes crashing down altogether, in the face of a crisis. That can be one of the greatest blessings in disguise.

Chapter 3

Going Within #3: Taking Stock of our Relationships

Avoiding Relationship?

Part of genuinely going within, during a period of crisis, is to take stock of our relationships. During a time of crisis, it's natural—and at times, even *required*—to internalize, to seek space or distance from others. But even in such situations it is not possible to avoid relationship. This is because relationship is as much a mental and emotional reality as it is a physical one.

A useful two-word inquiry in this regard, is *Avoiding relationship?* In this context, 'relationship' does not necessarily refer to primary relationship, but rather to our relationship with life in general. A good metaphor here is that of a closed fist. To contract inwardly, to recoil from life and from others, is to avoid forward movement, growth, and expansion (excepting those occasional times where brief periods of inward 'hibernating' or retreat is appropriate). To relax the fist into an open hand (to extend the metaphor) is to let go and to embrace the reality of our interrelatedness and interdependence with life.

As a poetic illustration of this interdependence, the renowned Vietnamese Zen master Thich Nhat Hanh once said that in a sheet of paper is found a cloud. This was so, he pointed out, because paper comes from trees, and trees cannot grow without water, which comes from clouds.

The point is sound. We live in an interlocking matrix of interdependence. A crisis tends to force us to become aware of that. In general, a crisis makes us more aware of the real status of our relationships, on what ground they truly stand.

We are always in relationship. There is no avoiding that reality. Even if we 'socially' or 'physically distance', or renounce human societies and retreat to a mountaintop hermitage in Tibet, or to a forest meditation hut in Thailand, or to the subarctic tundra of Canada or the Outback of Australia, we are still in relationship with the cosmos around us. The air we breathe, the food we eat, the ground upon which we sleep, the life-forms that pass before our eyes and the stars over our head, all are the objects of existence that we are in perpetual relationship with no matter how disconnected we may wish to be from human beings. And inwardly, we are also always in relationship with our thoughts, feelings, memories, sensations, and so on.

Deeper stages of realization may yield the understanding that relationship between separate entities is a mental construct—all is interconnected—but we have to guard against the tendency to want to get to that understanding too quickly; to spiritually bypass. Far better is to address the reality of our interrelatedness, both inwardly, and outwardly, especially when it does *not* seem to be seamless.

Most 21st century people are not cut out for the life of the renunciate or even the life of the loner. Some very creative people can do well on their own for extended periods, absorbed in their creations, but even these people must come to terms with their internal 'hardware' that, as a human being, has them wired for social interaction. Even those sincere spiritual seekers who do lengthy meditation retreats, must still negotiate their relationships with their fellow travelers, and must still come to terms with the relationships of their own personal history.

People at the opposite pole of the solitary person, those highly codependent types who have great difficulty being alone for any significant length of time, are not necessarily better off when it comes to dealing with relationship, despite all their time spent with others (and often accumulate more 'karmic entanglements').

The Decision to Prioritize Truth: Know Thyself

To truly take stock of our relationships, and to intend to live a life that is awake, is based on the decision to prioritize truth. That is the fundamental idea upon which all self-realization is based. Put simply, no inner work will amount to anything if we do not make the realization of truth the most important thing in our life. 'Truth' in this sense should not be understood as some philosophical point, let alone the 'truth' that pertains to religion, politics, or even science. It is, rather, the 'truth' of understanding who we are. It is the maxim *know thyself*, made famous via Plato and Socrates, and sourcing from the ancient temples of Delphi. In the context of relationship knowing ourselves is so important, because we can only know or understand another person to the extent that we know and understand ourselves.

However, even if we do decide to prioritize truth—to *know ourselves*—our work has only just begun. For in the very act of formulating this intention, we quickly find out just how sincere we are. For everything unlike this intention will soon bubble up in our mind, clamouring for attention and disputing our decision to know ourselves. In general, we can refer to these counterforce tendencies as *resistance*.

Resistance to self-understanding in the context of relationship takes several forms. Below are some of them:

1. **The Fairy Tale.** This can be understood as the sum of all pictures in our mind relating to our various attachments, and what we think our best possible life could look like. Invariably the fairy tale is based on various input programming we've received from what surrounds us— the ideas of others, the messages of popular culture, and so on. The fairy tale is egocentric, that is, is based on an idea that has our separate and distinct identity at the center of everything, and receiving things from the world—attention, recognition, status, love, material

comfort, and so on—in such a way that involves minimal or no true giving on our part. And even if our fairy tale features activity and giving on our part, it still tends toward fantasy and complete avoidance of the actuality and responsibilities of here-now. It always takes place somewhere else, 'long ago in a galaxy far, far away' as the tagline from *Star Wars* had it. And when other people do not conform to our fairy tales, as is invariably the case, we resent them, or dismiss them, or try to control them or avoid them. During a crisis, this all becomes accentuated. Our fairy tales get magnified, as their tenuous connection to reality becomes increasingly clear.

2. **Laziness**. Laziness is an extraordinarily formidable foe that arises in response to the intention to be awake. Its essential message is 'I am not inspired.' It speaks to a fundamental lack of energy, an attraction to painless sleep, unconsciousness, and ultimately death. It is the part of us that can't be bothered. It contains elements of deep resentment, and a strong desire to be taken care of, to not have to be responsible. It says, in so many words, 'I have nothing to do with this mess, and I do not really want to be here. Either take care of me or leave me alone.' During a crisis, this can become very problematic, because for the best state of mind, being proactive is usually required. This proactivity may involve tackling a practical matter externally, or it may involve developing an internal discipline, such as during times when one is spending more time alone.

3. **Pride**. Pride is, at its core, the belief that we are special. The deepest fear that most people encounter when considering the idea of self-discovery is the notion that they will disappear as an individual, and more to the point, that

they will lose their specialness, that which defines their personal identity. It is the fear of finding out that one is not that special that repels people most effectively from more deeply embracing the idea of waking up. And yet, going beyond more childish notions of specialness is often the very thing that opens us up to a deep and fuller connection with life. (People walking some sort of 'personal growth' path, and especially those drawn to more esoteric avenues, can be prone to this, typically born out of a rebellious urge that they often carry within).

4. **Vanity.** Vanity is self-absorption—the myth of Narcissus in all its many faces. It is the deep and perpetual fascination with our own drama, as if it is the only drama going on in the world. In our vanity we tolerate (more or less) the existence of others, but we are not much interested in them—unless they somehow reflect or relate to some issues that have to do with us. Then suddenly we are interested in them. But we are not truly interested in them; we are interested in us, and they are, again, a means to an end. A crisis can be strong medicine that forces us to encounter our vanity. The antidote is to begin to consider the reality of others more than we typically do.

Some Principles of Conscious Relationship

1. *You cannot be alone.* Even if living on a desert island, you are not alone. Even if isolated in a home, you cannot be alone.

2. *There is no such thing as 'the One'—that one special person who will magically make everything better for us.* There is only reality, your life as it is. The relationship you are in, provided there is absence of abuse, it almost always

good enough to engage the process of mindful relating. Your partner then becomes your 'learning partner', or your 'healing partner'. This can apply to friendships as well. Belief in the special 'One' is sometimes call 'One-itis', a type of psychological malady that causes us to live in a fantasyland or perpetual waiting room, waiting for something that never shows up.

3. *Mindful relating—or simply the intention to be more honest in relationship—often begins with a crisis.* This is usually some disappointment with codependency or a practical or large-scale event out of your control.

4. *Opposition reveals your true face.* A 'full moon' occurs when the Moon is in opposition to the Sun, with the Earth in between. In opposition, the Moon shines brightest. Similarly, when someone opposes us, or seems to have opposite characteristics to us, we often are provoked into revealing our 'true colors' (the good and the bad). This is sometimes called the 'coincidence of opposites'. It offers an explanation as to why people who seem opposite to us in certain ways can be strangely compelling. We are all seeking wholeness, and the 'opposite' type of person can seem to invite that possibility of achieving wholeness, via relationship of some sort with them.

Indeed, we tend to be attracted to opposites, much like magnets. Our work then is to take responsibility for the part of us that is attracted to our opposite, instead of just blaming them for being so different from us. When two people are very similar, they can become good friends (if other factors line up). Primary partners, however, often have tendencies that are opposite, something typically called 'chemistry' (though 'alchemy' is probably more accurate). Because of this, primary partnership can be very good grounds for seeing ourselves more clearly (instead of just focusing on how your partner is different); if we are willing to be accountable for our thoughts and feelings, instead of blaming or expecting our partner to parent us.

5. *We must learn to love truth more than our fantasies and attachments.* If we don't prioritize awareness and the willingness to honestly look at things, we tend to repeat old, self-defeating patterns. Our lazy mind and its refusal to look at itself—it's refusal to truly *go within*—results in us stubbornly looking for the (non-existent) magical 'One' who will make it all better.

Chapter 4

Going Within #4: Shadow Work

*Everyone carries a shadow. The less it is embodied in the individual's cons\-
conscious life, the blacker and denser it is'.*
C.G. Jung[6]

An essential element of going within during a time of crisis is to investigate the more hidden parts of our mind—our personal blind spots. This is one of the most important things to appreciate about the inner journey. 'Going within' is not about hibernating in some comfort zone sanctuary inside where we will be insulated from everything. On the contrary, it is more like staying in your home and cleaning up your files, dusting your bookcases, and deep cleaning the bathroom. It is a process that can be challenging but ends up rewarding on many levels.

In the language of modern psychotherapy, looking into our 'blind spots' is typically called 'shadow work'. What follows is an overview of some of the main principles of shadow work. But first, a brief story.

It was in 1985 that I first traveled to Asia. I went there to undertake multiple pilgrimages. When I arrived in India, via Thailand and Japan, I wandered about the north of the country visiting several places that had long caught my fancy—to the Taj Mahal, then to the so-called 'tomb of Jesus' in Kashmir (based on the Muslim legend that he had survived the crucifixion and lived to an old age in northern India), and further into the mysterious lands of the north. While wandering in the Tibetan highlands and the Himalayan region of Ladakh—called the 'Moonland' for its sparse landscape that lacks any significant vegetation—I stayed for a while in a cheap ramshackle hotel on the outskirts of the backwater town of Leh.

One night, I wandered out into the countryside. It was a moonless night, and overhead the stars were vivid, the thin, greenish veil of the Milky Way visible in a land free of urban-light pollution. I must have been walking on the dirt road for about an hour. I was in a valley flanked by enormous mountain ranges that ate up one-third of the sky, visible as menacing silhouettes all around me. Passing by the odd simple wood house or hut, I suddenly became aware of a low growling sound. The entire area was permeated with silence, making this strange growling more vivid and disquieting.

I stopped and looked around in the general direction of the growling. I could make out a dark mass, perhaps 20 feet away from me, from which the sound was emitting. I squinted into the darkness. As my eyes adjusted, I recognized what it was. I had once owned a pure-bred dog and at that time had made a study of dog breeds. What was growling at me was a Tibetan Mastiff, a very large black dog used by Tibetans and Ladakhis mainly as a guard dog. In appearance it is a type of cross between a Rottweiler and a sheepdog. Tibetan Mastiffs are notorious for their aggression and protectiveness. They are huge and intimidating, and when in attack mode, they resemble the deity Mahakala, a fiery guardian who eats demons for a living.

The dog was clearly not leashed, no humans were in sight, and it was a stone's throw away from me, growling intensely. Its eyes glinted demonically in the cold starlight. There was little doubt in my mind that this dog could seriously harm me and probably kill me if it wanted to. Relying mainly on some primitive instinct I slowly backed away, lowering my gaze. I kept walking in reverse. The dog began to follow me, matching my pace, all the time growling. This must have gone on for at least five minutes, me slowly walking in reverse, the dog following about 20 feet away, like some menacing shadow. At a certain point I turned 180 degrees and began walking, at a normal pace, away from the animal. He followed for a short while, still growling, then when satisfied I was leaving his territory, lost interest and went back the way he came. You could say, he simply did his job.

That dog was a good metaphor for the human 'shadow', the dark side of our nature that when denied, repressed, or otherwise frustrated, can manifest as a nasty foe, but when worked with, understood, and integrated, serves as a guardian or enforcer of boundaries, as well as providing the raw energy for creative expression.

One of the greatest challenges with facing into our shadow elements is the tendency to think that it will mean something about us in the ultimate sense. If I face into my anger, or my jealousy, or my fear, it must mean that that is the kind of person I am, and that is all there is to it. In my own case, it took me some time to get the hang of shadow work, and to really understand what it is about.

The problem, in my case, was that I was still regarding shadow-work as a type of procedure—like fixing a car or a medical operation—after which I would somehow be 'cured' of my condition. But that view was what lay at the heart of the problem in the first place. The constant desire to be something *other* than what we are just leads to a perpetual state of self-rejection.

Carried on long enough, self-rejection morphs into self-loathing, which is a difficult rut to escape from. Many people locked into self-loathing commonly end up on antidepressants or seek escape via other forms of altered consciousness (drink, drugs, entertainment, compulsive sex, turning their smart phone into their primary partner, etc.), or they resort to blaming and attacking others. Even more to the point, we humans seek escape in highly co-dependent relationships. In general, we seek to numb out and distract, thus remaining largely asleep to our greater possibilities. We use relationships to 'medicate', to dull the pain and fear of encountering who we actually are. We use *other people* as the means to escape from ourselves.

Shadow Work

The term 'shadow', as I mean it here, was first coined by C.G. Jung, the highly influential early 20th century Swiss psychiatrist and scholar. Jung had originally been a close student and associate of Sigmund Freud—in fact, he was being groomed to be Freud's successor—but broke away from him while in his late 30s, owing to significant differences in viewpoint and theory. Freud, of course, was a revolutionary thinker in that he was one of the first to understand the mechanism of *repression*, that is, the ability we have to block, deny, or simply be unaware of large parts of our mind and personality. Jung added other elements to Freud's view of the psyche in ways which were ultimately unacceptable to Freud, but he also developed the notion of the shadow (originally called by Freud the 'id'), leading to more comprehensive methods for working directly with these shunned and concealed parts of our nature.

The value of knowing our shadow side can't be overestimated. This is due to a simple reason. We humans have the remarkable ability to 'see' our hidden parts in the characters of other people. This ability to see in others what is also (or only) in us, is known in psychological language as 'projection'. *You* are angry, not me. *You* are weak (manipulative, jealous, fearful, take your pick) not me. (For the record, there is a 'positive' projection, where we see qualities in others that we admire that are latent or active in us, something Plato called 'admiration' and identified as a key to successful relationship. Here, however, we're more concerned with looking at the disowned negative aspects, as they are the problem children of our minds).

Most relationship erosion and breakdown are due to the function of negative projection, based on the failure to clearly see our shadow side. We typically blame others for behaviors and qualities we also have—or at least, hold the potential to display. Further, we tend to dislike—or, as commonly, are strangely attracted to—people who remind us the most of our disowned parts. Because we don't tend to see our disowned parts clearly (or at all), we also usually don't clearly see why we dislike, or are attracted to, someone. 'I just do' or 'I just am' are the typical thoughts.

Deconstructing our projections takes effort. Mental laziness can be a problem here. Moreover, we have an investment in not looking into our mind as this involves being accountable for who we are. If we are to be accountable, that makes it more likely that we would forgive and release those people from our past (parents, ex-partners, disowned friends and colleagues, etc.) who we believe have wronged us, or who are to blame for our misfortunes in life. Many of us don't wish to grant that forgiveness, and therefore have reason to resist looking within and taking responsibility for our projections.

'Shadow-work' comes down to a radical acceptance of both our outer character and essential nature. It does not (or at least, should not) make excuses for self-sabotaging character tendencies, nor dismiss them as unimportant in the greater context of our overarching 'spiritual' selves that are presumably beyond all this. Shadow work is based on unqualified honesty and the willingness to break past internal censors that stop us from telling the truth. When embracing shadow work, we must let go of the need to be seen as good, pure, or special in any way. We must truly embrace our human frailties. In a sense, we must confess our humanness, thereby moving past the obstacle of pride.

The idea that we are fragmented, conflicted beings with parts of our personality struggling with other parts is basic to the human condition. However, the crucial point to grasp is that no amount of personal growth trainings, techniques, or hours of processing, deep breathing, or meditation will resolve the core issue if we don't learn to recognize and acknowledge the less flattering parts of our character and stop trying to separate ourselves from them (as if such a thing can really be done anyway).

To own our shadow qualities does *not* mean to be directed by them. Hate and anger and jealousy and fear will direct *us* if we are in the business of rejecting them. A disowned part of our personality will start pulling the puppet strings in all kinds of ways. The key to shadow-work is indeed ownership, but this ownership cannot just be mouthed, it needs to be lived.

The whole point of shadow work, and of any sort of transformational process work, is not to 'improve' ourselves, but to see and understand the nature and degree of our self-rejection. In that sense, it is much more akin to deep self-acceptance. The very urge to change our self is what is causing the problem in the first place. This urge can be called 'neurotic seeking'. It is what compels many people to seek out therapy or personal growth, so it should be understood as a natural motivating force. However, it easily becomes a problem. Used in the best way, the 'urge to change' grows into a mature curiosity about our character and essential nature.

All therapy and meditation ultimately reduce to self-observation. Not in an inwardly contracted, self-congratulatory, self-absorbed fashion, but in a manner that enables us to stop apologizing for who we are, and, by extension, to begin to understand others better as well.

Practical Shadow Work

Shadow work may be said to proceed along a few basic lines. A good writing exercise is as follows:

1. Write out a list of qualities you most dislike in others.
2. Write out a list of qualities you most dislike (or disliked) in family members.
3. Notice how any of these qualities seemed to show up in your primary partner relationships or close friendships or important work colleagues.

4. Finally—and this is the important step—notice how many of these qualities can be found in yourself, even if only in a more rudimentary form. For example, you don't like weakness when you see it in others. Is there some part of yourself that you suspect, or secretly know, can be weak in given situations? And so forth.

The idea behind noting these matching parallels is to begin the process of reclaiming projections. It should be understood, however, that 'reclaiming projections' has nothing to do with granting license to others to repeat bad behavior. When you understand shadow work, you begin to understand that it has nothing to do with other people at all. It is really about going within and knowing yourself. That knowledge gradually leads toward greater empowerment and freedom.

Confession and Radical Acceptance

The basis of shadow-work is confession. But not the typical confession that is often motivated simply by guilt. The confession we speak of here has more to do with dropping defenses and pride. When we go beyond defensiveness and pride, we can directly see the ways in which we have contributed to problems by shortcomings of our personality. 'I was impatient, intolerant, unkind, vengeful, weak and compliant, overly-negative, complaining to excess, more interested in myself than my partner, I saw them mainly as a body, or a source of security, or as a surrogate mother or father', etc.

Initially we may frame a confession in past terms—'I *was* unkind', etc. Confession becomes more potent when we see the ways in which we *are* this way, not just how we were in the past. A common way to try to wriggle out of present-time confession is to suggest or claim that one is now beyond these tendencies—'I used to be this way', and so on. It is highly unlikely that we have rooted this pattern out of our personality, even if we fancy that we have been working on ourselves for some time. More likely we have merely spent time out of primary relationship, in which the lack of a consistent mirror in our lives has lulled us into believing that we are 'not that way anymore'. Or, more cleverly, we blame our difficult manifestations of behavior on a past partner—'*they* brought it out in me'. Or, we are in a long-term relationship in which both parties have formed a tacit contract with each other to not 'stir the waters', to avoid dealing with deeper matters, and in so doing, to go to sleep.

Confession is the ignition to get the engine up and running, but the car is not going anywhere without a full acceptance of the very traits we are identifying in confession. This step is often confusing to people. They may think that by confessing their negative tendencies these same tendencies will now magically transform. They rarely do by the power of confession alone. They require, initially, a full acceptance. This full acceptance is generally known as *ownership*. To 'own' impatience, for example, is not just to tell the truth about one's impatient tendencies, but also to step into them fully and inhabit them from within without any recoil or self-condemnation.

To 'inhabit' a shadow tendency from within has nothing to do with indulging it or allowing it to direct one's life, or worse, causing you to ill-treat others. Shadow traits only direct our lives when they are not seen and identified, and not properly owned. They need to be named, in order to be tamed. Once 'tamed', we see the deeper point—the shadow is not something separate from us. It *is* us. It just waits, sometimes patiently, sometimes impatiently and even destructively, for us to see that point.

The result of this journey is self-acceptance, and a reduction in hostility—whether that hostility be directed toward others (grudges) or, more commonly, toward oneself (self-esteem issues, self-doubt, depression). Shadow qualities, when integrated (owned) become the fuel and fire that warms and drives our life. A person who is in ownership of their shadow qualities is not just trustworthy, they are also capable of a warmth and creative power that can truly contribute to the growth of humanity. They are not just living for themselves. They are living for the greater context and vast universe in which they are immersed.

Chapter 5

Going Within #5: Meditation

Meditation Requires Resolve

Anybody who seriously tries meditation sooner or later finds out that it is not easy. The main reason meditation is challenging is that our minds tend to be confused and undisciplined. For most people engaging in meditation does little more than make them directly confront the reality of their already confused and undisciplined mind. It is something like taking a close look at a room in your house you have been avoiding for a long time that you already know is a mess—and doing nothing about it except looking carefully at your mess. Invariably, you find out that the mess is worse than you thought. And moreover, to keep looking at the mess is disheartening, boring, and potentially depressing.

Much of our life consists of distractions. This is very true in modern high-tech times, but it was true in older, simpler times as well. We humans have always avoided looking within, instead being inclined to getting lost in distractions.

The Buddha, when he worked out his system for enlightenment 25 centuries ago in northern India, nailed down the main reason for human mental suffering. He defined it via the Pali word *tanha*, which translates loosely as 'craving'. This 'craving' is essentially the desire for states of existence that will somehow relieve us of our inherent discomfort, self-rejection, and fear of life. These always lead to suffering because external matters are always changing (impermanent). By clinging to them, we set ourselves up for disappointment and pain.

If we fear what is within us, or if we deeply believe that we are somehow 'missing a piece' within that can only be found in other people or the things of the world, then it's natural that we will seek externally for that thing—and also seek, at all costs, to avoid facing the emptiness that we fear is within. And that is why we seek distractions. And that is why sustained meditation can be so hard, because it removes those distractions. It takes our 'distraction-drug' away, and sooner or later we feel the withdrawal effects.

I have done several long-term meditation retreats over the years. These have often been punctuated by periods of deep frustration, where I had to face into the reality of who I was, and the kind of mind that I had. In these retreats I would often experience the full reality of how locked into my mind I had become. I would become vividly aware of the fact that I was living in a *story* that had been crafted by my mind. I was the playwright, and the solo actor, of my own script.

This is arguably the main condition of humans. In a sense, we are all 'locked into our minds'. We experience reality via the filters of our mind. Sound arguments have been advanced by some of the deepest thinkers in history that *all* we experience is the reality of our mind—its thoughts, perceptions, memories, projections, and the feelings and sensations it generates in concert with our bodies. In short, our version of reality—our *story*.

Even our experience of another person is filtered via our mind. We have *ideas* about things, and we have *ideas* about other people. Unfortunately, it's common to experience little beyond those ideas and the expectations, projections, unrealistic views, and fears that they typically generate. Much of the time we live in a kind of self-preoccupied bubble—the bubble of our personal story and its version of things.

Getting Out of the Story

The path of going within and waking up to a greater view of reality is founded on the premise that we must somehow acquire the ability to see beyond our thoughts—to escape the limitations of our personal consciousness—and to directly experience reality beyond the projections and delusions of our psyche. But how do we do this? How do we escape from a story that we ourselves have authored?

There are different approaches here. The most time-honored has been the practice of meditation, which essentially reduces to gaining the discipline to slow down the movement of thought to witness it more clearly. With practice, it becomes increasingly clear that our deeper identity is *not* the content of the thoughts our mind generates, but rather, the witnessing awareness itself. All the great wisdom traditions of the world, be they from the East or the West, are ultimately based on this understanding, though they call this 'witnessing awareness' by different names.

With practice, as one settles into the witness mode, the mind becomes increasingly stable, with a corresponding effect on moods and emotions. We begin to see our story-version of reality for what it is, a story. Deeper states of peace and a seamless connection to the moment-by-moment movement of reality become very possible. The 'enlightened' individual is one who stabilizes and abides in this state, although they will typically experience fluctuations in their consistency to abide in the witness—'good days and bad days', as it were.

That said, there are very distinct ways to go wrong with meditation practice. A common form of this was characterized by the famous Tibetan Buddhist master Chogyam Trungpa as 'spiritual materialism', which is closely related to the more current term, 'spiritual by-passing'. The basis of this kind of by-passing is the unwitting usage of meditation as a means of distancing oneself from deeper shadow feelings (anger, hate, fear, jealousy, lust, etc.) In that regard, meditation become more a type of *medication* in which we dissociate from deeper feelings and shadow thoughts.

How do we avoid by-passing? There are different approaches to the matter of 'rolling away the stone' of the unconscious mind to gain deeper access to its contents. Here it should be noted that the unconscious mind has barriers and walls for perfectly good reasons. For example, if a person harbors significant repressed wounds connected to early-life traumas, then it follows that these painful memories indeed need to be 'sealed away' if we are to function adequately in our day to day lives. It is not always right or appropriate to knock those walls down.

Makyo

The issue of 'spiritual bullshit' is one that any sincere truth-seeker sooner or later encounters (or 'phony holiness', as the more religious version has it). As a good lead-in to this topic, it's helpful to look at the Zen concept of *makyo*.

Makyo in Japanese literally means 'the devil in phenomena'. Technically, it has to do with various states of mind that arise in sustained meditation, especially elaborate visions that, in some respects, herald deeper meditation practice. These visions, or other states of mind, are ultimately to be let go of however, because they are mind-constructs, even if impressive ones. On a more subtle level, what *makyo* refers to is the seductive power that the mind has to pull us away from our pursuit of here-now wakefulness. When we sit in meditation, or when we attempt to truly go within, we inevitably face almost endless distractions. We get diverted, and in so doing, we fall into elaborate dream-worlds.

We live during a time of chronic attention-deficit and data overload. The glut of available information via endless advances in communication technology means that the average person is now bombarded by all sorts of information that can harm their capacity to truly pay attention to one thing at a time. There are no more secrets in almost any field of learning, including the wisdom traditions. Everything is available. But does it make any difference?

In meditation, as in life, this can become a problem because the temptations are magnified. As Oscar Wilde once lamented,

'I can resist anything but temptation'. We live in the Golden Age of temptation. We are not only distracted and tempted by outer events — the craziness of a world with nearly eight billion people, the temptations of social networking or the latest Netflix binge-watch that calls to us — we are also distracted and tempted by our thoughts that reflect the sheer busyness of our lives. Accordingly, it becomes more important to become increasingly discerning about the distinction between *makyo* and reality. Between imagination, and what is really going on.

Solitary meditation can seem like a lonely pursuit. Our guide is nothing else but a deep desire for peace, wisdom and truth. Nurtured, this desire becomes passion. And our passion for going within, if we stick with it, soon becomes a vehicle by which we start to open doors in our mind, and experience the benefits of our practice: physically, emotionally, mentally, spiritually.

If we are truly interested in knowing ourselves, we need to go beyond distractions and their power over us, and we need to remember, daily, *what really matters*. The main point to understand is that our real nature is not an experience. It is a state of being, something like the vast, empty sky overhead, that can only be obscured, but that is always there, waiting for us to return to it

Some Meditation Techniques

It is easy to gain access to material, both in printed books and online, on basic meditation techniques, so these will not be covered here in detail.[7] Just a few basic methods are suggested, as follows.

Self-Remembering

Self-remembering, in one form or another, lies at the heart of inner work. It has gone by various names over the centuries within the various spiritual traditions, but it always boils down to the practice of maintaining an elevated state of awareness throughout one's daily life activities. Self-remembering is based on the idea of divided attention. In typical semi-conscious living, our attention flows outwardly, toward the object we perceive. It is a one-way movement of attention, from us, to the object. The less alert, the less conscious we are at the time, the more we are aware of *only* the object, and nothing else. (This is, of course, the basis of being caught up in the external 'glitter' of reality, everything from the dazzle of a charismatic person, to the dazzle of a cause we identify with).

A good example of this occurs in our dreams at night. Typically, our dream state is governed by a lack of self-awareness during the dream. All that is 'real' are the objects (things, people, etc.) of our dream. This is why we do not know that we are dreaming at the time, because there is no substantial self-awareness. Thus, we wake up after and realize that it 'was only a dream'.

In divided attention, what we are endeavoring to do is to 'split' our attention two ways, so to speak. We try to keep our attention on the object of our perception (say, a tree), and, at the same time, we remain aware of ourselves—'I am'. We attempt to remain aware simultaneously of both self and tree. Accomplishing this is an act of self-remembering. In the beginning the practice may seem just intellectual, a forced and artificial mental effort that probably will not be sustained for very long. With consistent practice it becomes easier and more natural and can be done for longer periods of time. Persisted with, we can reach a state where we are naturally remembering ourselves much of the time. As our ability with the method progresses, it becomes less and less a detached mental exercise, and more and more an alive, sensory experience of being *present* in our environment and experiencing the moment more vividly.

To self-remember is to be *present*. Lack of presence is akin to operating in a kind of auto-pilot state. The main purpose of self-remembering is to begin to learn to experience reality free of mental projections and of the cloud of 'daydreaming' that obscures our ability to be truly here. Self-remembering, persisted with, leads to a quieter mind, a mind that thinks more economically and efficiently and is able to let go and relax when appropriate.

It should be understood that with all meditation methods, including self-remembering, we are not trying to force the mind to be still. Trying to will the mind to be silent usually leads to just repression of thoughts and feelings. Self-remembering is not about repression. It is rather a practice that allows us to be more involved in our life in a real fashion, while being able to see things more clearly and truthfully as well. We can practice while driving, eating, going to the washroom, walking, etc. In the beginning it is good to try this method when not engaged in anything serious, but over time we can do it in increasingly complex situations.

Exercise #1 (Self-remembering): Attempt to remember yourself as the one who is having this thought, or the one who is having this feeling, body sensation, etc. — that is, hold the sense of 'I am' whenever possible throughout your daily activities. This does not mean that you can't engage in regular activities or thinking that requires your full attention. It simply means that you remember the sense of 'I am' when having such thoughts, feelings, and so on. In the beginning self-remembering can seem like a tedious mental exercise, in that you have to make a mental effort to remember, 'I am'. But over time this 'I am-ness' becomes less and less a disconnected thought, and more an overall sense of embodied presence, and one that becomes easier to remember.

Exercise #2 (Self-Observation): In selected situations throughout a typical day, practice simply observing yourself, without comment or attempt to change anything at all. Just try to catch yourself doing and acting and thinking and feeling and behaving however you may be in any given moment or situation, but don't try to change anything—just bear witness to yourself, be as aware as possible of yourself. This exercise can be a bit difficult in the beginning and as such is best at first to practice in simple, routine situations. These may include when you stop at a red traffic light, standing in line somewhere, interacting with a grocery clerk, etc. In all these situations, remember whenever you can to simply observe yourself.

Exercise #3 (Vipassana): Vipassana is an old Buddhist meditation technique believed to originate from the time of the Buddha, and probably even before that. It is very simple and effective, yet requires discipline, commitment, and patience. Begin with twenty-minute sessions, increase up to one hour as you feel ready. Seated comfortably, back straight but not rigid, take a few deep breaths, and relax into yourself. Then, locating the breath in either the pit of the belly, or at the tip of the nose (choose one location or the other, and then stick with it), simply follow your natural in-out breathing rhythm with your awareness. No matter what, keep your awareness on your breath. Simply stay with the breath. At first, you will forget the breath again and again, as you drift off into thought-dreams. That is normal, try to not get frustrated or self-reproachful, simply keep returning your awareness to the rise and fall of the breath. As you follow the breath bear witness to whatever is happening, but keep your awareness anchored to the breath. This method is excellent for focusing and grounding, as well as clearing the mind and centering within.

Chapter 6

Going Within #6: The Retreat

The events of the global pandemic of 2020 have resulted in some extraordinary changes in society, foremost of which, on the practical level, has been separation (distancing), and isolation. The lessons and challenges that go with this are more or less obvious and need not be repeated here. Need for proper self-care and clear communication with others is at a premium. But it is also natural in such circumstances for some to explore the idea of a retreat, either formally, or in a more casual fashion. Not all have the means or the desire to do such a thing, for sure. But for those that do, this is a good time. What follows in this chapter are some guidelines for undertaking a retreat, as well as remarks on a prolonged solitary retreat undertaken in Nature.

The Way of the Psychonaut

From May 20 to June 30 of 1988—a period spanning forty days and forty nights—I did an intensive solitary experiment that involved fasting, communing with Nature, extensive meditation, self-examination, dream-work, and trance-work. The retreat did not include any usage of entheogens or any other direct mind-altering substances. The first 10 days I fasted (juice and water for 3 days, water only for 6 days, and one 'dry day' with no food and no water). The last 30 days I took regular, though simple, meals. The retreat took place in an isolated cabin in the forests of the Coastal Mountains of British Columbia. This was an inner and outer operation that required significant commitment to complete.

My choice of a forty-day retreat was, at the time, based mainly on practical expediencies. It was the maximum amount of time I could take off from work. I was, many years later, intrigued to discover that the English word 'quarantine' derives from the Italian word *quarantina*, meaning '40 days'. During the mid-14th century, when the Black Death was ravaging parts of the world and especially Europe, some sort of plan was implemented (in Croatia, initially) requiring visitors to be isolated for 30 days ('trentine') to see whether symptoms of the disease would show. In the 15th century, when periodic outbreaks occurred, it was first lengthened to 40 days in Venice, from whence arose the term 'quarantine'.

The cabin I used belonged to a friend of mine with whom I had arranged a barter with for usage of it. The cabin was situated in deep woods about two-thirds of the way up the south face of a mountain. The retreat had been undertaken under the loose guidance of a mentor I had briefly had at that time, a mystic who worked with trance-mediumship and related forms of shamanism. For my retreat he'd suggested I be near either ocean or mountains. I opted for the latter, having always felt a kinship with mountains.

A sustained retreat undertaken for inner work—whether that be called a meditation retreat, a vision quest, a magical retirement, or by any number of designations—is common to many wisdom traditions. Perhaps the most sustained and developed of these retreats are found in Asia, and in particular, in Tibetan Buddhism. That is natural, as the chilly plateaus north of the Himalayas, as well as the forbidding mountain ranges themselves, have long been thought of as sanctuaries to those more extreme seekers of inner truth sometimes known by the modern term 'psychonaut'. I have spent time in Tibetan Buddhist monasteries, though perhaps ironically, my own deepest psychonautic experiences took place in my native Canada.

The word psychonaut—and the accompanying term psychonautics—stem from the Greek terms *psyche* (mind/soul/ spirit) and *nautes* (navigator/sailor of the seas). Therefore, a psychonaut is technically a 'navigator of the seas of the mind/

soul/spirit'. Or, more simply, a navigator of the inner worlds — standing polar opposite to the astronaut, who is the navigator of the outer stars (from 'astra', Greek for 'stars').

The prolonged spiritual retreat has not been limited to Tibetan traditions. Certain Christian hermitages have abounded with legends of cloistered monks and tales of the solitary Desert Fathers, along with Islamic (Sufi) mystics, Jewish renunciates, and Hindu sadhus who wander the land as mendicants, and other hermits devoted solely to inner practices. Also renowned is the North American Indian vision quest.

In the Western esoteric tradition, and especially within the area known loosely as ceremonial magic — doubtless one of the more obscure, least-known, and most irrationally feared pathways to self-knowledge — there exists the formidable practice known as the Abramelin Operation. This is a 'magical retirement' known mainly via the notorious book *The Book of the Sacred Magic of Abramelin the Mage*. This book, written in the 15th century by one Abraham of Worms (a town in central Germany), was first brought to public notice by Samuel MacGregor Mathers, one of the three founders of the Hermetic Order of the Golden Dawn. Mathers' published a translation in 1900 of a French copy that specified the retreat as being 6 months long, although subsequent work by the German researcher Georg Dehn, working with older German manuscripts, established that the retreat specified by Abraham was in fact intended to be 18 months long.[8]

In the Christian tradition, the 'Temptation of Christ' is a cornerstone of the legend of Jesus, based on his 40 days and nights in the desert, in which he is confronted by Satan, the great tester. What is less commonly known is that Elijah and Moses also undertook 40-day retreats. In all three cases, they fasted for the entire 40 days. That degree of effort was beyond my capacity and purpose — 10 days of fasting, out of the 40 days of my retreat, was more than enough for me and about all I was willing to attempt.

The various categories of retreat, including the tradition most commonly associated with them — in increasing order of difficulty — look something like the following (of course, one could pick any random number of days; these are some of the most renowned).

1. Three-day retreat (basic).
2. Four-day vision quest (Native Amerindian). Best undertaken in Nature.
3. Ten-day meditation retreat (Theravadin Buddhism, usually employing vipassana meditation).
4. Three-week meditation retreat (Theravadin and Zen Buddhism).
5. Forty-days retreat (tradition of Moses, Elijah, Jesus, and the Desert Fathers).
6. Six-month retreat (Abramelin Operation, Mathers' version).
7. Eighteen-month retreat (Abramelin Operation, Dehn's version).
8. Three years and three-month retreat (Tibetan Buddhism).
9. Ten-year retreat (Tibetan Buddhism).

The purpose of any retreat based on legitimate psycho-spiritual practices is to purify one's mind and open it to, and align it with, its highest potentials. These 'highest potentials' are typically defined in transcendent terms, because they are deeply intangible, and thoroughly experiential. Words may be recorded (or situations filmed on your smartphone), but nothing substitutes for the direct experience. To cite the old Zen analogy, words or images are 'fingers pointing toward the Moon', with the Moon representing, in this metaphor, the unqualified, undefinable *isness* of consciousness and presence.

A basic recommendation of any sort of retreat is to keep a journal or diary of it. In my case, I kept detailed notes, scrawled in pencil in two simple notebooks. When I began the retreat, I intentionally brought no timepieces or calendars with me. Each day, I never knew what time it was and the only way I knew what day it was, was by my journal entries. And even then, I lost track once or twice.

The retreat was a focused experiment intended to tap deeply into the unconscious mind, and in so doing, to experience the subtle, transpersonal realms of spirit. For this, I had to find ways to disengage the conscious intellect. Bringing no timepieces or communication devices of any sort was part of that. Yes, cellphones—though primitive versions of them—did exist back in 1988. Like most people then I did not own one. The times we inhabit now are very different, in that it is more difficult to disengage from our network of contacts. In current times, should one take a cell phone to a lengthy retreat, especially in Nature? The answer is yes, for safety purposes. However, the idea is not to use it unless absolutely necessary! That requires significant discipline.

Disengaging the conscious intellect for an extended period is hard work. As it happened, when I was in the cabin I found a cheap paperback on the history of Western philosophy, which was comfort food for my complaining intellect. I indulged myself for a few afternoons of the retreat and read the book. Aside from that, I stayed with the program, which consisted of the following:

1. Six to eight hours daily of sitting meditation. This included various forms of trance-induction work, both waking and hypnagogic, alongside classic forms of witnessing meditations such as vipassana and Zen *koan* work, and invocations of higher mind (or 'holy guardian angel', to use the Western esoteric term).

2. Daily strenuous hikes in the forests of the local mountains, including at night with no flashlight. This included

scaling a nearby mountain, a modest 4,000-foot peak, and extended meditation on its summit (which was cool and still snow-encrusted even in June).

3. Daily journaling, recording in detail experiences in meditation, hikes, and nightly dreams.

4. Art therapy as a means to connect with both archetypal and personal ancestral spirits. Each day I drew extensive colored images of faces that would arise in my mind during the meditations. (Art is a very potent and underrated method for accessing the unconscious, as it works via visual symbols, the language of the unconscious).

5. Diet, which was very basic, free of meat and refined sugar, but enough to keep my energy up.

6. Strenuous manual labor, such as digging ditches.

The month-long retreat, though mainly concerned with the inner world, was punctuated by a few memorable outer events. These included being confronted by a vicious stray dog (I was not injured) and getting lost in the forest on one of my night hikes. The latter was indeed memorable. I never understood prior to then just how dark a mountain forest becomes in the dead of night. As much as my human eyes struggled to adjust (and I had flawless vision then), I could barely see my own hands in front of me. I recall I had to get down on the ground and crawl my way through the forest in order to orient myself. I eventually emerged into a dried-up creek and was able to trace that route back to the cabin. I arrived back at what I estimated to be around 3am. I couldn't sleep, so energized was I by the ordeal. My entire body-mind was on fire, doubtless the effect of adrenaline flooding the body in the face of what my mind judged to be a significant threat to survival.

More than one person has gotten lost in the wilds before, never to be seen again. David Paulides, in his compelling (and controversial) '411-Missing' books, documents hundreds of unsolved cases in North American national parks alone over recent decades. The reason it is so easy to become disoriented in a forest is because nothing is symmetrical, unlike our largely symmetrical towns and streets. A forest is shrouded, organized chaos. It is easy in a darkened forest to not realize that you've circled back to where you started, and therefore not really gone anywhere (a theme well portrayed in the classic campy 1999 horror flick *The Blair Witch Project*).

In addition to the physical adventures, I also experienced various of the following:

> A deep sense of connection with what I can only categorize as ancestral spirits. Part of this was connected to an assignment I had been given by my shaman-mentor to draw faces that would appear in my mind in my meditations. This in turn seemed to form a kind of link to the personality, which in turn opened the door for a connection that I can only describe as ultimately healing.

However, not all such experiences were pleasant. On one occasion—in a *dream* state, I emphasize—I was 'visited' by a mechanical-type creature who pressed painfully on my lower back, and then suddenly whisked me away to a spacecraft that was orbiting Earth. On this craft I was ushered down some hallways into a strange room. It was a generally unpleasant experience. After a hiatus I eventually found myself back on the couch in the cabin, with a weird buzzing sound around me and a strange metallic taste in my mouth. Over the next few minutes, I came fully back into my body. Strange experiences such as these, which become easier to experience during prolonged isolation in Nature, make it clear that psychoactives are not needed if the discipline of meditation is applied, along with the luxury of sufficient time to go deep.

Other equally bizarre paranormal and mystical experiences

visited me during my time in the cabin. Much of this was accompanied by periods of deep emotional purging. In some ways it was like being turned inside out. The force that drove these experiences was the outer and inner quiet I was entering. The forest is not a particularly quiet place, especially in June, when all sorts of creatures are stirring about. But as my mind became increasingly quiet, I began to tune into the natural silence all around me. The forest was buzzing with life, but it was also strangely silent at the same time, utterly free of the constant psychic-chatter of human society. After a while, I began to realize where the silence was coming from. It was simply part of Nature, but it was also the natural state of the mind when free of distractions, and when the flow of thought has been slowed down sufficiently via disciplined daily meditation.

It can be surprisingly hard to commit to, let alone organize, an extended retreat. What follows are some of the most common roadblocks.

Impediments to Retreat: Survival, Fear, Lack of Desire for Truth

1. Survival. Undertaking a significant retreat usually requires considerable practical planning. It can be surprisingly complicated to arrange. This is one of the reasons why such retreats—especially for those longer than two weeks—are often easier to undertake when under the age of 30, or over the age of 60. The years of adulthood from approximately 30 to 60 are generally the busiest years, in which our lives are more complicated, weighed down by entanglements, obligations, and responsibilities difficult to get away from.

2. Fear. The word 'fear' is left alone and generic here, as it can apply in many directions. The most common fear is in the psychological category, and basically reduces

to the fear of being alone. For retreats in wilderness or general nature locations, this fear can be enhanced. It may also involve fears of disappearing or dying without being noticed or found. These fears can be reduced to core-beliefs of personal unworthiness or unimportance or inherent unlovability.

3. Lack of Desire to Go Deep. This is perhaps the most significant barrier, because if the longing for deeper truths is not there, then the motivation for tackling the two impediments above will not be there either. Essentially, the desire for truth—or, put alternatively, the love of truth—has to overcome the psychological fears and practical obstacles.

There are of course many examples of mystics who have undertaken lengthy retreats, from the time-honored classic stories of the Buddha (his six years in the forest, though he did consort with various teachers and yogis during that time), Jesus, Milarepa, and Ramana Maharshi. Perhaps one of the more remarkable, and well documented, more recent examples is that of Tenzin Palmo (born Diane Perry in 1943), an English ordained Tibetan Buddhist nun who was subject of Vickie Mackenzie's book *Cave in the Snow: A Woman's Quest for Enlightenment*.[9] Her example is extraordinary because she spent twelve years in a remote Himalayan cave, three of which were spent in meditative isolation. During those three years she grew her own food and only slept three hours a night while sitting upright in a wooden box.

Such feats of discipline are beyond most people, and rarely necessary. But the power of extended time in solitude, and especially in Nature, should not be underestimated. My own retreat had a specific focus, that of aligning with my higher nature, while at the same time facing the demons within—those buried in my subconscious, those that are echoes of my family tree and its history, and those of deeper karmic tendencies. In my own case, my 40 days culminated in a spectacular experience of ecstasy as I established communication with a 'spiritual force' that I can only, to this day over three decades later, regard as transcendent. The communion with this 'force', utterly independent from my ego-mind, was extraordinarily real, as real as the keyboard upon which I type. That said, the main point I stress here is that an extended retreat of any sort—be it for 6 months or 6 weeks or 48 hours—will result in some sort of direct insight into the deeper recesses of one's being, provided one truly commits to the process. In longer retreats, this direct insight very commonly manifests in some extraordinary ways.

The above describes a fairly ambitious retreat, that in my case was, in the end, very much worth it. For most people, a shorter retreat is both more practical and all that is needed. Here are some general guidelines for a 3-day retreat:

1. No communicating with anyone. This is important. Best is to leave aside your phone for the three days (unless going into wilderness) If you have it on you, try to keep it shut off the whole time. Avoid checking social networking, etc. Tell someone close to you, like a family member, where exactly you'll be, and that you'll be out of touch for three days.
2. Writing is okay, reading is not recommended. Journal out your thoughts.
3. Keep a dream diary.
4. Artwork. Take some paper and colored pencils or markers and draw images that come to your mind in meditation.
5. Meditate daily.
6. Juice fasting is best. If you do eat, keep it very light.
7. Don't oversleep. It's not supposed to be a hibernation, but rather a wakeful retreat.
8. Exercising. In some retreats, you stay indoors, so obviously

this exercising has to be constrained by that. Pushups, sit-ups, jogging on the spot, or simply a long walk outside in the early morning is ideal.

Chapter 7

Going Within #7: Night School

During any period of retreat—or any period of crisis that leads one to undertake a retreat—the notion of attending 'night school' becomes an important idea to consider. This night school, however, has nothing to do with sitting in a classroom, physical or virtual. It has rather to do with exploring the inner dimensions via dreamwork. The following chapter explores some of the theory and methods of dreamwork (or 'dream yoga' as it is sometimes called) and in particular one of the less well-known variants of it, lucid dreaming.

The inner work can be undertaken not only during the daytime waking hours, but also during the night when our bodies sleep. The purpose of such work is to advance our understanding of the nature of our consciousness. Our time on this Earth in one lifetime is relatively short, so it makes sense to use what time we have to deepen our practice. Dreamwork is making use of the approximately 30 percent of our lives we spend asleep (which for the average lifespan amounts to about twenty-five years).

Lucid Dreaming

Lucid dreaming is *conscious* dreaming, that is, a dream where we know that we are dreaming. (The technical term for this is 'consciously self-referencing'). There are different levels to that knowingness; some lucid dreams are profoundly vivid, where our conscious awareness is virtually equal to waking state reality; others are somewhat vague dreams in which we assume that we are aware that we are dreaming, but only realize upon waking that this 'awareness' was in fact rather dim. Most lucid dreams seem to be of the middling sort, where we clearly recognize that we are dreaming during the dream but realize upon waking up that our lucid-dream state consciousness was slightly different in contrast to our waking state.

For example, it can be common to have a lucid dream of walking through the rooms of one's home, in which one seems to be fully aware that one is dreaming, but upon waking realizes that one did not consciously register the fact that the furniture in one's home was different in the dream in contrast to how it is in actual waking life. This may be mainly due to the sensory effects of the physical body being disengaged during the dream state, making it very difficult for the brain to accurately replicate our actual physical surroundings. Equally so, it may be that our mind is re-creating our physical bedroom on a subtle plane, in what amounts to a different version of it.

Etymologically, the word 'lucid' has nothing to do with dreaming. It derives from the Latin word *lucidus* which means 'clear', 'bright' or 'shining'. The term 'lucid dreaming' was first coined around 1913 by the Dutch psychotherapist Frederik van Eeden, but it was not picked up seriously until the 1970s–80s by Celia Green, Ann Faraday, Steven LaBerge, and others, all of whom used it to describe a dream where we know we are dreaming. Of course, dreams where the dreamer knows they are dreaming are not a 20th century development. Certain very old shamanistic cultures, such as the Australian Aborigines and their 'dreamtime', had advanced practitioners. Tibetan dream yoga, which in part concerns lucid dreaming, was mentioned as far back as the 800s CE. Even St. Augustine, in a letter dated to 415 CE, mentioned a lucid dream he had.

The challenge that all wisdom-traditions have always had to tackle is the issue of what to do with the rational mind when seeking to explore the 'inner planes' (or deeper levels of mind). Carlos Castaneda—who himself wrote extensively about lucid dreaming in his (probably) fictional 1972 work *Journey to Ixtlan*, referred to the means of quieting the mind as 'stopping the internal dialogue' so that a fuller awareness can emerge.[10] That is a theme one finds in most traditions that explore altered states of consciousness, such as trance and dream state.

Conventional psychoanalytic dream-interpretation involves using the rational mind to try to make sense out of symbols, which is worthy enough, but lucid dream work aims to take it a step further to the point where we can *interact and converse with our own symbols*. That is, we can interact with the deeper parts of our mind; we can dialogue with normally inaccessible realms of our being. We become our own live, interactive dream book.

The Stages of Sleep

Most people follow the following sleep patterns, which have been understood since the 1950s:

> We begin in stage one, light sleep (which registers as theta waves). This is that strange space we fall into, in which someone may wake us and we are convinced that we were not actually sleeping. This stage generally lasts around five to ten minutes. We then go into stage two, which is about twenty minutes long, in which vital signs slow down. We then enter stage three (where delta waves begin), leading to deep, dreamless sleep.[11]

In some wisdom traditions (such as Vedanta) the stage of dreamless sleep is accorded great importance, recognized as synonymous with a purity of consciousness in which there is no subject-object duality—'consciousness without an object' it is also called. According to some of these traditions the reason we usually have no recall of this state upon waking is that our sensory attachments (via the physical body) and the deeply engrained belief that we are a separate bodily entity overrides our memory of the pure non-duality of stage three sleep, resulting in no recall—'I was not there' is the conceptual conclusion we form and simply take for granted. And in some respects, this is true: we as we typically experience ourselves in normal waking consciousness were not in fact 'there'. (Something clearly *was* there, because we return each morning when we awake).

We typically spend about a half-hour in stage three sleep. Curiously, stage three is followed by a return to stage two sleep, where we spend another twenty minutes or so. From there, we jump straight to stage four sleep, known as REM ('rapid eye movement'). This is the stage where most dreaming, including lucid dreaming, takes place. By the time we get to REM, about ninety minutes have elapsed. So, if we go to sleep at midnight it is unlikely we will dream much until about 1:30 a.m. (Dream-like visions happen commonly in stage one sleep, but this is not full dreaming). We then repeat this cycle several times through the course of the night. The first entry into REM sleep lasts only a short time, about ten minutes, but each subsequent ninety-minute cycle results in us spending longer and longer times in REM sleep. For one going to sleep around midnight, the best chance to induce a lucid dream would be around 4:00–5:00 a.m., or toward the end of the sleep cycles in the morning, sometime between 6:00 and 8:00 a.m. As a result of this there is a correlation between lucid dream work and enough sleep. The probability of experiencing lucid dreams increases if we get at least six to eight hours of sleep, simply because the later REM stages tend to last longer.

Dream Recall

No dream work is possible without first developing dream recall—the ability to properly remember dreams. In most cases this takes some time along with consistent practice, although many people can dramatically improve their dream recall within a few weeks.

The simplest practice is to keep a notepad by the bed, and to write down our dreams as soon as we wake up in the morning (or middle of the night, if we prefer). Most people soon find out that the only real way to make this work is by having a note pad on our night table and jotting down dream details *as soon* as we wake (memories of dreams tend to fade rapidly). In the beginning it does not matter if most of the dream details are forgotten by the time of waking. Even jotting down a few memories of the dream is enough to begin strengthening dream recall. Most find that without the note pad there is little hope in getting dream recall happening. Because dream memories are so tenuous, it is helpful to have an 'anchor' to fix the memories. Note-pad writing is, for most people, such an anchor. Once we have begun to recall some dreams, we can set about attempting to induce a lucid dream. (Speaking into a recording device is also possible, provided you sleep alone).

Methods for Inducing Lucid Dreams

One of the best methods for inducing lucid dreams is to set some sort of task before going to sleep that serves to trigger lucidity during dreaming. A good example was Castaneda's method of attempting to find one's hands in one's dream—that is, setting the intention, just before sleep, that we will see our hands in our dreams. Also possible is to suggest that we will recognize absurdities while dreaming (such as our car suddenly flying, and so on—these are usually known as 'dream signs'). Some people have lucid dreams merely by thinking about them during the day or reading material about them. However, most need to apply some sort of practice that involves setting an intention immediately prior to falling asleep. The following uses the 'hand-finding' technique.

1. Before going to sleep, we suggest to ourselves that tonight, in our dreams, we will find our hands. That is, we will have a dream where we remember to look at our hands. This pre-sleep suggestion need not take long; about thirty seconds to suggest 'tonight, I will see my hands in

my dreams'. This should be accompanied by visualizing holding the backs of our hands up to our face.

2. Once we find our hands in our dream, this acts as a mnemonic device to trigger the realization that we are in fact dreaming. Prior to this happening we may have several dreams in which our hands are peripherally present (for example, dreaming of driving a car, or of opening a door—or in current pandemic times, of washing our hands), which we realize only upon waking and reviewing the dream. Eventually we will have a dream where we remember, *while still dreaming*, that we are in fact dreaming.

3. A common result of realizing that one is dreaming is to suddenly awaken from the dream. To prevent this, the best thing to do is to keep looking at different objects in the dreamscape, but not to focus on anything for too long.

Some of the other main lucid dream induction methods (in addition to finding the hands, or feet, etc.) are as follows:

1. MILD (Mnemonic Induction of Lucid Dream): The idea here is that when we awaken immediately after a dream (in the middle of the night, or in the morning,) we are to recall the last dream we were having, and then mentally relive that dream—with the added factor of *imagining* that we are awake in the dream as we replay it in our mind. When we fall back asleep again, we stand a better chance of having a lucid dream. (Those who have seriously tried this method have reported a dramatic increase in lucid dreams, to the point where they can occur almost nightly).[12]

2. WILD (Wake-Initiated Lucid Dream): Here we try to retain unbroken consciousness as we fall asleep. This generally only works in late sleep REM stages, that is, after we have already slept for several hours. Early morning hours (or

afternoon naps) tend to be best for this approach. Methods to use can involve focusing on the breath, images arising in the mind, overall sense of the body, and so forth. These act as an anchor for self-consciousness, which can then be retained even as the body falls asleep.

Tibetan dream yoga focuses on WILDs, generating them via a visualization method—for example, visualizing a black dot, or a white dot, or a particular geometric or spiritual symbol—while falling asleep. Retaining our focus on the visual image helps to sustain awareness as we pass into sleep. We then end up with the interesting experience of our body being asleep, but not our awareness, as we pass into REM stage. This is sometimes experienced as 'sleep paralysis' (and is typically disturbing if we do not understand what is happening). Many quietly suffer from 'sleep paralysis' without understanding it; such people may have a marked capacity for dream-work.[13] On the physiological level, all that is going on with sleep paralysis is that our brain is inhibiting physical movement because we are entering REM stage. To dream of jumping out a window, and actually getting up and jumping out the window, would obviously not be good, so sleep paralysis is simply the brain's way of protecting our body while we dream.

3. WBTB (Wake-back-to-bed): The idea here is to abort our sleep a bit; that is, if going to bed at midnight, then wake up after five or six hours, stay awake for an hour or so, then go back to bed and use MILD or WILD method. This tends to result in the highest possibility of inducing a lucid dream.

Noticing Universal 'Dreamsigns'

'Dreamsigns' is the term coined by Stephen LaBerge[14] that refers to 'dream absurdities', those events that typically occur in dreams that would be nonsensical, or otherwise out of place, in our waking life. Once recognized in a dream they can trigger the realization that we are in fact dreaming. There are several dreamsigns that are universal and seem to be true for most dreamers[15]:

1. *Electronics fail*: Electronics usually do not work or do not work correctly in dreams. No one knows why, but it could be because modern technology is so complicated the dreaming brain cannot duplicate it.
2. *Incorrect lighting*: Many times, the lighting for a situation will not be correct. It will either be too dark or too light. Another noticeable dreamsign is that attempts to change the lighting do not work. Quick changes in light require recalculation of colors and shadows, which seem to be too much work for the dreaming brain. Shadows may also look distorted or go in the wrong direction.
3. *Deformation*: Animals, people, objects, and scenery often look strange in dreams. The object of attention tends to be larger than everything in its surroundings. Noticing anything misshapen should be an obvious dreamsign, however it tends to be the hardest one to pick up on.
4. *Illegible Text*: Reading and writing tends to be difficult or impossible in dreams. If text seems blurry or jumbled together, it should be a clear dreamsign. Text may also constantly change and never appear to be the same message twice. This also works with digital clocks.

With practice we can learn to notice these dream signs, which then trigger us into the realization that we are dreaming.

Tibetan Dream Yoga and the Practice of the Night
Some schools of Tibetan Buddhism and the shamanistic Tibetan Bon tradition developed dream work to very high levels. In

English these systems have been called Dream Yoga. Below is a simple technique adapted from the Tibetan Buddhist tradition[16]:

1. Before going to sleep, send out a few positive thoughts to others, wishing them well, etc.
2. Remind yourself that you will remember your dreams tonight. Tibetan tradition generally recommends that you lay on your side—women on their left side, men on their right side.
3. Repeat the following simple prayer:

May I have a clear dream. May I have a lucid dream. May I understand myself through dreaming.

Repeat this several times with sincerity (either out loud, or internally). Then visualize a symbol in your throat. The symbol should be visualized in luminous red. You can use the English letter 'A'. Hold this visualization for as long as you can as you fall asleep.

Tibetan dream yoga has a much deeper purpose than merely generating lucid dreams. The key idea here centers on the word *rigpa*, which translates as 'awareness' or 'knowing' and refers to our intrinsic nature, our true being, free of the confusions and projections of the mind. The inner work essentially boils down to differentiating *rigpa* from typical conceptual thought. The practice of dream yoga, in particular via the process of falling asleep consciously (what LaBerge called the 'WILD' method, and what Namkhai Norbu calls, in its more realized teaching, 'the Practice of the Night'), is a means by which to train ourselves to experience pure non-duality or unobstructed consciousness (*rigpa*), which is our 'natural state'.

We can do this via dream yoga because each night when we fall asleep, we are entering into a state of non-dual consciousness. We do not typically recognize it because we are so identified with objects and thoughts that we are unaccustomed to experiencing our consciousness *without an object to focus on*. By training ourselves to fall asleep while visualizing a symbol (such as 'A'), we can realize the state whereby our consciousness merges totally with the object. There is no longer 'me' as distinct from the object; there is simply pure consciousness, recognizing itself as separate from nothing.[17]

Levels of Lucidity

Having a legitimate lucid dream is generally an unmistakable experience. Occasionally one may hear people who say, 'I think I've had a lucid dream, but I'm not sure.' In those cases, it is almost a certainty that their dream was not fully lucid (or possibly, their memory of it was distorted, resulting in the doubt). In most cases there is not the slightest doubt. The contrast between an average dream and a lucid dream is akin to the contrast between sleep and waking up in the morning (or between a black and white photo, and one in color). The only difference is that this 'waking up' occurs while we are still in REM sleep and the dream is still going on.

It helps to recognize that there are several levels of lucid dreaming. The following six-level model is adapted from Robert Waggoner's *Lucid Dreaming*[18]:

1. *Pre-lucid*: This is the phase of noticing 'dreamsigns', what would be absurdities or impossibilities in waking life.
2. *Sub-lucid*: A vague recognition that you are dreaming but lacking strong self-awareness. This might take the form of 'my car suddenly flew in the air, so I knew the dream could not be real'.
3. *Semi-lucid*: this is the first lucid-dream proper level. Here we know we are dreaming, but we continue to follow the dream-plot without consciously altering the dream in any significant way.

4. *Lucid*: This stage is like the last, that is, we know we are dreaming; however here we make a conscious effort to control the dream by changing things in it.

5. *Fully lucid*: This marks a more advanced stage in which not only are we aware that we are dreaming, but we also have full awareness of what is going on in our physical life. That is, we can consciously recall and think about events going on in our physical life—'yes, I know that even though I am dreaming now, I have to pay this bill today, or that person spoke to me yesterday', etc.

6. *Super-lucid*: This is a higher energy level where all conventional interests are dropped in favor of spiritual states of consciousness. For example, you might be lucid dreaming of walking in the marketplace. Suddenly you dissolve the marketplace in your mind and direct your attention to higher realities that might involve states like unconditional love, transcendent wisdom, communication with advanced beings, etc.

That does not mean, of course, that only a dream where willful autonomy is exercised is a true lucid dream—for example, it is entirely possible and natural for an experienced lucid dreamer to 'do nothing' and allow events to unfold in the dream. I once had a lucid dream where I realized that there was in fact nothing I wanted to actively pursue in the dream. So, I simply sat down on the ground, went into lotus posture (a posture I can't do in my physical body—but, the dream body is flexible!) and went into meditation. After a period, I 'woke up' into my physical body.

The outline above is helpful to refer to, for a number of reasons. First, it suggests a natural evolution to how we experience lucid dreams. Psychologically, the biggest fear people tend to have around stage four lucidity (exercising control of the dream) is that somehow, they will find out something about themselves that they would rather not know. For example, in exercising control in a lucid dream we may find out that we have certain desires, etc., that might surprise us. We may discover that there is a tyrant in us, or a manipulator, or we may find out that we have certain fixations, or we may unearth strong emotions or sexual desires, and so on. The reason all these may surface into awareness is precisely because the 'laws' of the dream world are much less constricting and limiting than the laws of physical reality. (Gravity being one simple example—as most people know, we can fly unaided in the dream world). Either way, our dreams reveal the hidden sides of our nature. According to the wisdom traditions, dreams expose these hidden parts, in the same way that death does—both for the living, and for those going through the death process.

There is an old expression: 'to find out the truth about someone, just give them power'. In a lucid dream that power is potentially there, and we naturally seek to exercise it to some degree, not for the purposes of going morally astray, but simply for the purposes of self-discovery. This is necessary because we do not transcend the limitations of personal ego until we first see it, assume responsibility for it, and understand it. Dream work can be excellent in that regard in that all the risks associated with physical reality are not there. For example, if we decide to fly to Mars in a dream because the desire to do so is there, we need not repress the desire as we would have to do in physical reality, which does not support unaided space flight. More than one person lost their life via LSD seeking to exercise a similar desire, which could have been harmlessly experienced in the lucid dream state.

There are many benefits to dreamwork and especially lucid dreaming. Here are a few:

1. *Economizing time.* We spend much of our life unconscious, asleep in our bed. As the Tibetan master Tenzin Wangyal

once observed, we need not undertake a traditional three-year meditation retreat; we need only undertake dream work over the span of one decade, during which time we will spend about three years in sleep anyway. Why then not use this great amount of time that is otherwise simply forgotten?

2. *Bolstering self-esteem and counteracting a negative self-image* (the latter which, alongside chemical imbalance, is a prime factor in depression). A common result of dream work is a greater sense of inner accomplishment. Lucid dreams tend to yield a healthy sense of empowerment, especially in the beginning. As one goes further, a greater humility can arise as well, in that one begins to glimpse the vastness of the greater Self. This is especially so when we encounter 'independent agents' (as they are sometimes called) in a lucid dream. This is an element of the dream that appears to be completely out of our control. An example may be encountering some people in the dream, asking them questions, and they all replying in unexpected ways just as if they were fully discrete entities. In an ordinary dream that is commonplace, but in a lucid dream it is a very different kettle of fish. It can be both fascinating and humbling in a healthy way, particularly if some sort of control in the lucid dream state has been achieved.

3. *Creative realizations.* A common result of lucid dreaming is to realize creative potential. There are reports in the literature of lucid dreamers creating music in their dreams or solving difficult problems. The Tibetan master Namkhai Norbu, after years of dream yoga practice, reported that during one retreat he had lucid dreams where entire texts containing lengthy teachings were revealed to him. He reported that even upon waking he could still briefly read the texts that appeared in front of him before they faded.

4. *Therapy.* Lucid dreams can be powerful ways to resolve

negative dreams or nightmares, by learning how to confront the issues in the dream and even dialogue with them. To dialogue with dream elements is something the famous psychologist Fritz Perls, founder of Gestalt Therapy, based much of his work on (though doubtless some tribal cultures have done this before, via ritualistic re-enactment). This can be done in waking life as a form of therapy, but also in a lucid dream. For instance, during a typical dream in which one encounters a 'monster' of some sort, lucidity enables one to remember that it is just a dream, and thereby overcome a fear. This in turn becomes a powerful metaphor aiding us in understanding the mind-constructed nature of our experience of reality in our regular waking life—including our deepest fears.

5. *Spiritual realization.* Via lucid dreaming we can begin to see that all phenomena are interdependent with mind, which is in turn the underlying secret behind all manifestation practices (i.e., mind—in theory—can alter certain elements of reality). However, the deeper point is that through lucid dreaming we can begin to see directly into the nature of 'naked awareness' (*rigpa*) itself and see how it lies at the basis of all phenomena.

Dreams show us how all phenomena are passing, or, in a sense, 'plastic'. This in turn helps us to reduce our attachment to worldly matters. According to many wisdom-teachings it is excessive attachment to objects and possessions that lies at the root of most of our suffering in life. By learning how to be a bit less attached, we can go deeper into the nature of reality. In that sense, dream work is a kind of initiation chamber into the deeper mysteries of self. Additionally, there is the possibility in lucid dreaming of communicating with unknown or previously unrecognized sources of information and wisdom, which can even include deceased relatives or other icons of wisdom.

As touched on above, concerning the issue of control in lucid dreams, a significant element that ultimately appears in almost all cases of lucid dreaming is that of the 'independent agent'. This often happens when a degree of facility with lucid dreaming is reached, and we might become a bit overconfident, perhaps even arrogant, in our ability to manipulate dream elements. At that point a common occurrence is that something happens in the dream that is out of our control. A hand may come out of nowhere and grab us, or a person we are talking to might respond or act in some way that shows that we have no control over them, and so on. This idea was shown with the 'agents' in *The Matrix* movie series, where certain elements of the constructed world of the supercomputers could not be controlled—namely, Agent Smith and his cohorts—as they operated from a different 'order' of reality. These same elements have their equivalents in lucid dreaming as well and may be seen to be part of the greater Self that is training the personal consciousness, bringing greater balance to it.

Lucid dream work can at times be frustrating, but as with all spiritual practice, the key is to persist. The book *A Course In Miracles* has a wise expression: 'An untrained mind can accomplish nothing'. This is certainly true with lucid dreaming as well. It requires a strong intention to succeed, a firm decision to not waver from the intent to awaken deeper levels of awareness, whether in the dream state (lucid dreaming) or in the waking state (self-remembering). This kind of inner work is ideally suited for any time requiring us to truly *go within*.

A Few Concluding Remarks

The journey within has never been easy, but it is a journey that we all must face at some point or another. A crisis can often be a horrible event, for many obvious reasons. It can also be a transforming event—cooking us in fires of purification that lead to a metamorphosis, the emergence of something new and fresh. My hope for any reading this book is, if beset by your own challenges, that you use some of the ideas in these pages to make sense of the difficulties around you and in the lives of others you care about.

Appendix

A Note on Trance States

Any extended period of going within via meditation or solitary retreat opens one up to the reality of the various states of consciousness our minds are capable of. Most forms of traditional esoteric work such as certain advanced yogic practices, ceremonial magic, and shamanism deal comprehensively with these states, though not typically with modern scientific or psychological terms.

The 20th century Romanian scholar Mircea Eliade defined shamanism as 'archaic techniques of ecstasy'.[19] In order to understand this, it is helpful to realize what exactly is implied by 'ecstasy'. Typically, this word is associated with some sort of euphoric or blissful experience, but in fact the word more precisely is connected to specific *altered states of consciousness*. The word derives from the Latin *extasis* and the Greek *ekstasis*, meaning an 'entrancement' which may involve positive or negative experience that is in some way 'out of normal experience', i.e., altered. It was only in the 17th century that the word, as used by some mystics, began to be associated with blissful or rapturous states where the mystic communed with the divine. There is a close connection between the words 'ecstasy' or 'ecstatic' and the words 'charisma' or 'charismatic', the latter of which stem from the Greek *kharisma*, meaning 'divine gift'. Shamans in most traditional cultures are thought to be summoned or visited by the divine, i.e., bestowed with a divine gift—exactly the original meaning behind the word 'charismatic'.

There is a further precise meaning of the word 'ecstasy', and this relates to the idea that the altered state of consciousness is brought about by the complete involvement of subject-consciousness ('I') with object-consciousness ('that'). Any creative person deeply involved in their craft, any person immersed in a moment of profound intimacy, any thinker seized with a profound insight arising from strong concentration, may have had a glimpse, or more, of this state of consciousness. Intensive dance, dreams, visions stimulated by entheogens, or even on occasion injuries or accidents, can provoke this state. But more commonly it is something cultivated by disciplined practice.

There is a parallel for the shamanic state of consciousness in classical yoga, called *dharana*, or concentration. The key element of this state of mind is that it ultimately involves a profound letting go, a relaxation in which the mind slows down to a rate that hovers between typical waking consciousness and sleep. This level — the 'crack between the worlds' — is the doorway to the realm of shamanic experience. It begins with concentration but ends with a shift in which the conscious ego is no longer in control. It is precisely this that allows access to the vaster realms of experience that are typically filtered out by our normal waking selves.

It's helpful to understand all this in terms of the accepted Western model of brain waves ('neural oscillation' is the technical term) and their various levels.

Gamma Waves: These are neural oscillations of around 40 Hz (Hertz, or cycles per second) though they range between 25 and 100. This level is not yet well understood, although tests have been done with trained meditators yielding some evidence that unified states of consciousness — a type of 'shared trance experience' — between separate individuals may be possible at this wavelength.

Beta Waves: These are found in the 12.5 to 30 Hz range. This represents typical 'waking state' consciousness. Logic, reason, typical 'clarity of mind' is found in this range. However, the upper ranges of Beta are also associated with stress, anxiety, and the rapid thinking typical for more restless or even disturbed states (including depression).

Alpha Waves: These represent the frequency range of 7.5 to 12.5 Hz. and are associated with wakeful relaxation. Most light meditation, 'spacing out', and other 'guided meditation' forms of personal growth are connected to this range. It is here where positive affirmations work and positive suggestion is most beneficial. In other words, to reprogram our minds we have to learn to relax. Conversely, negative programming (or subliminal advertising that is manipulative in intent) also works in this range.

Theta Waves: These occur in the 4 to 7 Hz range and are associated with deep relaxation, drowsiness, sleepiness, and meditation. (Of course, 'sleepiness' and 'meditation' are not synonymous—in fact they are opposites in terms of alertness. However, both hold in common a deep relaxation of the body and slowing down of brain waves). This is also the range of REM sleep and most typical dreaming.

Delta Waves: These are associated with frequencies below 4 Hz, and deep dreamless sleep (non-REM). (This does not mean that the Delta Wave state necessitates all loss of consciousness. Highly trained meditators or esoteric practitioners and certain other individuals have demonstrated capability of retaining awareness while entering the Delta state. Traditions of non-duality, such as Advaita, define this state as basic to the fully enlightened condition, based on the idea of consciousness without an object—i.e., the subject and what the subject is aware of have collapsed into Oneness).

The doorway to the 'shamanic state of consciousness' is found largely at the Alpha and Theta border (7-8 Hz), with deeper states occurring exclusively in Theta. Experiments have been done suggesting that rhythmic drumming ('sonic driving') at a rate of about 4.5 beats per second is optimum for aiding in inducing the Theta brain wave state (corresponding to the Theta Hz range). It is here that significant insights, spontaneous visions, and potentially liberating realizations or creative breakthroughs can occur. This is also the doorway to the so-called 'out of body state' (OBE) and the 'wake induced lucid dreaming' (WILD) state explained in the last chapter. Many interested in accessing the Theta level of awareness stop short at the Alpha state, owing mainly to difficulties with relaxation stemming primarily from the fear of letting go of control. The following are important for consciously accessing the Theta state: clarity of intent, clearing the mind, letting go of control, and abandoning all expectations.

Notes

1. www.ncbi.nlm.nih.gov/pmc/articles/PMC6736881/ (accessed April 14, 2020).
2. www.cdc.gov/flu/pandemic-resources/index.htm (accessed April 1, 2020).
3. https://coronavirus.jhu.edu/map.htmlJohns Hopkins site (accessed April 1, 2020).
4. From Emerson's *Nature*, chapter 1. www.archive.vcu.edu/english/engweb/transcendentalism (accessed April 2, 2020).
5. *Human, All Too Human.*
6. C.G. Jung, *Psychology and Religion* (1938), p. 131.
7. Two previous books of mine, *The Inner Light* (Axis Mundi Books, 2014), and *The Way of the Conscious Warrior* (Changemakers Books, 2019), include descriptions of many basic techniques.
8. For the Mathers' version, easiest to consult is the 1975 Dover paperback edition. For Dehn's work, see *The Book of Abramelin*, Ibis Press, 2006.
9. Bloomsbury, 1999.
10. Carlos Castaneda (1925–1998), was a Peruvian-American writer who had a marked influence on young North American seekers, particularly of the 1970s-80s. He claimed to have met and been trained by an old but powerful Yaqui Indian *brujo* (shaman, or 'sorcerer' as he translated it), and subsequently documented this apprenticeship, and the teaching he later developed on his own, through twelve books. Castaneda's first four works, published between 1968 and 1974, are often recognized as his best. However, they were also shown, via the incisive analysis of Richard DeMille (*Castaneda's Journey*, 1976; *The Don Juan Papers*, 1980), and Daniel Noel (*Seeing Castaneda*, 1976) to have been almost certainly fictional accounts, despite his claims to the contrary. Nevertheless,

his works contain plenty of legitimate teachings and valid techniques of transformation, even though he seems to have followed in the old tradition of attributing these teachings to a fictional master and storyline, or at the very best a semi-factual one much embellished.

11. This stage used to be divided into two separate stages, 3 and 4; as of 2008 the American Academy of Sleep Medicine decided to discontinue the stage 4 category.

12. For a full description of these processes see Stephen LaBerge and Howard Rheingold, *Exploring the World of Lucid Dreaming* (New York: Ballantine Books, 1990). Also excellent is Robert Waggoner's *Lucid Dreaming: Gateway to the Inner Self* (Moment Point Press, 2009).

13. The evidence is that many experiences involving what are retroactively interpreted as 'intrusive entities' occur during this phase—everything from the so-called 'incubi' and 'succubi' of medieval lore, to the 'extraterrestrials' of the late 20th century 'abduction' literature. Whether these intrusive experiences all involve some meta-level of objective reality, or simple hallucinations, has of course been long debated.

14. LaBerge, *Exploring the World of Lucid Dreaming*, p. 41.

15. The following is adapted from the website www.dreamviews. com

16. See the writings of the Tibetan Dzogchen master Namkhai Norbu, especially *Dream Yoga and the Practice of Natural Light* (Ithaca: Snow Lion Publications, 1992).

17. It is worth noting in passing that there is an interesting correlation between the various stages of sleep outlined above, and the stages of the 'transition of consciousness' in the 'afterlife' realms as described in the *Bardo Thodol* (Tibetan Book of the Dead). The process of losing consciousness, the opportunity to recognize the true nature of the 'clear light', the loss of consciousness, and the subsequent 're-awakening' in the various 'bardos' within which one

experiences complex visions based on one's 'karmic traces' (usually ending in rebirth), corresponds roughly to the process of initial sleep, deepening sleep, REM stage where dreams arise that reflect our personality qualities, followed by eventual waking up. For a fleshed-out discussion of this, see Tenzin Wangyal Rinpoche, *The Tibetan Yogas of Dream and Sleep* (Ithaca: Snow Lion Publications, 1998), especially pp. 114–115; and Namkhai Norbu, *Dream Yoga and the Practice of Natural Light*, pp. 45–64.

18. Waggoner, *Lucid Dreaming*, pp. 276–277.
19. Mircea Eliade, *Shamanism: Archaic Techniques of Ecstasy*. First published in 1951 in France, numerous reprints and translations.

About the Author

P.T. Mistlberger was born in Montreal in 1959 and was educated at John Abbott College and Concordia University. He has worked as a transpersonal therapist and seminar leader since 1987, has founded several personal growth communities and esoteric schools, and is the author of six previous books.

A Natural Awakening

The Three Dangerous Magi

Rude Awakening

The Inner Light

The Way of the Conscious Warrior

The Dancing Sorcerer

TRANSFORMATION

Transform your life, transform your world – Changemakers
Books publishes for individuals committed to transforming their
lives and transforming the world. Our readers seek to become
positive, powerful agents of change. Changemakers Books
inform, inspire, and provide practical wisdom and skills to
empower us to write the next chapter of humanity's future.
If you have enjoyed this book, why not tell other readers by
posting a review on your preferred book site.

The *Resilience* Series

The Resilience Series is a collaborative effort by the authors of Changemakers Books in response to the 2020 coronavirus epidemic. Each concise volume offers expert advice and practical exercises for mastering specific skills and abilities. Our intention is that by strengthening your resilience, you can better survive and even thrive in a time of crisis.

Resilience: Adapt and Plan for the New Abnormal of the COVID-19 Coronavirus Pandemic
by Gleb Tsipursky

COVID-19 has demonstrated clearly that businesses, nonprofits, individuals, and governments are terrible at dealing effectively with large-scale disasters that take the form of slow-moving train-wrecks. Using cutting-edge research in cognitive neuroscience and behavioral economics on dangerous judgment errors (cognitive biases), this book first explains why we respond so poorly to slow-moving, high-impact, and long-term crises. Next, the book shares research-based strategies for how organizations and individuals can adapt effectively to the new abnormal of the COVID-19 pandemic and similar disasters. Finally, it shows how to develop an effective strategic plan and make the best major decisions in the context of the uncertainty and ambiguity brought about by COVID-19 and other slow-moving large-scale catastrophes. The author, a cognitive neuroscientist and behavioral economist and CEO of the consulting, coaching, and training firm Disaster Avoidance Experts, combines research-based strategies with real-life stories from his business and nonprofit clients as they adapt to the pandemic.

Resilience: Aging with Vision, Hope and Courage in a Time of Crisis
by John C. Robinson

This book is for those over 65 wrestling with fear, despair, insecurity, and loneliness in these frightening times. A blend of psychology, self-help, and spirituality, it's meant for all who hunger for facts, respect, compassion, and meaningful resources to light their path ahead. The 74-year old author's goal is to move readers from fear and paralysis to growth and engagement: "Acknowledging the inspiring resilience and wisdom of our hard-won maturity, I invite you on a personal journey of transformation and renewal into a new consciousness and a new world."

Resilience: Connecting with Nature in a Time of Crisis
by Melanie Choukas-Bradley

Nature is one of the best medicines for difficult times. An intimate awareness of the natural world, even within the city, can calm anxieties and help create healthy perspectives. This book will inspire and guide you as you deal with the current crisis, or any personal or worldly distress. The author is a naturalist and certified forest therapy guide who leads nature and forest bathing walks for many organizations in Washington, DC and the American West. Learn from her the Japanese art of "forest bathing": how to tune in to the beauty and wonder around you with all your senses, even if your current sphere is a tree outside the window or a wild backyard. Discover how you can become a backyard naturalist, learning about the trees, wildflowers, birds and animals near your home. Nature immersion during stressful times can bring comfort and joy as well as opportunities for personal growth, expanded vision and transformation.

Resilience: Going Within in a Time of Crisis
by P.T. Mistlberger

During a time of crisis, we are presented with something of a fork in the road; we either look within and examine ourselves, or engage in distractions and go back to sleep. This book is intended to be a companion for men and women dedicated to their inner journey. Written by the author of seven books and founder of several personal growth communities and esoteric schools, each chapter offers different paths for exploring your spiritual frontier: advanced meditation techniques, shadow work, conscious relating, dream work, solo retreats, and more. In traversing these challenging times, let this book be your guide.

Resilience: Grow Stronger in a Time of Crisis
by Linda Ferguson

Many of us have wondered how we would respond in the midst of a crisis. You hope that difficult times could bring out the best in you. Some become stronger, more resilient and more innovative under pressure. You hope that you will too. But you are afraid that crisis may bring out your anxiety, your fears and your weakest communication. No one knows when the crisis will pass and things will get better. That's out of your hands. But *you* can get better. All it takes is an understanding of how human beings function at their best, the willpower to make small changes in perception and behavior, and a vision of a future that is better than today. In the pages of this book, you will learn to create the conditions that allow your best self to show up and make a difference - for you and for others.

Resilience: Handling Anxiety in a Time of Crisis
by George Hofmann

It's a challenging time for people who experience anxiety, and even people who usually don't experience it are finding their moods are getting the better of them. Anxiety hits hard and its symptoms are unmistakable, but sometimes in the rush and confusion of uncertainty we miss those symptoms until it's too late. When things seem to be coming undone, it's still possible to recognize the onset of anxiety and act to prevent the worst of it. The simple steps taught in this book can help you overcome the turmoil.

Resilience: The Life-Saving Skill of Story
by Michelle Auerbach

Storytelling covers every skill we need in a crisis. We need to share information about how to be safe, about how to live together, about what to do and not do. We need to talk about what is going on in ways that keep us from freaking out. We need to change our behavior as a human race to save each other and ourselves. We need to imagine a possible future different from the present and work on how to get there. And we need to do it all without falling apart. This book will help people in any field and any walk of life to become better storytellers and immediately unleash the power to teach, learn, change, soothe, and create community to activate ourselves and the people around us.

Resilience: Navigating Loss in a Time of Crisis
by Jules De Vitto

This book explores the many forms of loss that can happen in times of crisis. These losses can range from loss of business, financial security, routine, structure to the deeper losses of meaning, purpose or identity. The author draws on her background in transpersonal psychology, integrating spiritual insights and mindfulness practices to take the reader on a journey in which to help them navigate the stages of uncertainty that follow loss. The book provides several practical activities, guided visualization and meditations to cultivate greater resilience, courage and strength and also explores the potential to find greater meaning and purpose through times of crisis.

Resilience: Virtually Speaking
Communicating When you can't Meet Face to Face
by Teresa Erickson and Tim Ward

To adapt to a world where you can't meet face to face - with air travel and conferences cancelled, teams working from home - leaders, experts, managers and professionals all need to master the skills of virtual communication. Written by the authors of *The Master Communicator's Handbook*, this book tells you how to create impact with your on-screen presence, use powerful language to motivate listening, and design compelling visuals. You will also learn techniques to prevent your audience from losing attention, to keep them engaged from start to finish, and to create a lasting impact.

Resilience: Virtual Teams
Holding the Centre when you can't Meet Face-to-Face
by Carlos Valdes-Dapena

In the face of the COVID-19 virus organizations large and small are shuttering offices and factories, requiring as much work as possible be done from peoples' homes. The book draws on the insights of the author's earlier book, *Lessons from Mars,* providing a set of the powerful tools and exercises developed within the

Mars Corporation to create high performance teams. These tools have been adapted for teams suddenly forced to work apart, in many cases for the first time. These simple secrets and tested techniques have been used by thousands of teams who know that creating a foundation of team identity and shared meaning makes them resilient, even in a time of crisis.